AFTER THE FALL

Dear Larry + Alyce
Here it is! We love you.
♡ Craig + Cyndy

AFTER THE FALL

A CLIMBER'S TRUE STORY OF FACING
DEATH AND FINDING LIFE

CRAIG DEMARTINO

WITH

BILL ROMANELLI

Kregel
Publications

Printed in the United States of America
13 14 15 16 17 / 5 4 3 2 1

This book is for everyone who has been knocked down until the only thing left is the belief that God has a plan through the valley. He does.

CONTENTS

PREFACE

"I am convinced that life is 10 percent what happens to me and 90 percent how I react to it. And so it is with you . . . we are in charge of our attitudes."

—CHARLES R. SWINDOLL

I never intended to write this book.

I never intended to be a person who others look at and think, "He's disabled." I never wanted the things that have happened to me. The broken neck, the nerve damage, the amputated leg, and the shattered but "saved" other ankle that hurts more than the amputated one—no, I never wanted any of it.

But I wouldn't trade any part of the experience for the world. Because I've been able to see that sometimes the greatest thing God gives us isn't healing, but the power to endure.

ACKNOWLEDGMENTS

This book has been a long time coming, but as always, God's timing has little or nothing to do with my timing. That's a good thing.

I couldn't have done this without Bill. My thanks goes out to him for listening while I rambled all those months on the phone, and to all the people who helped bring the story to life: Ms. Kyle Patterson, Eric Gabriel, Les Stobbe, Sally Stuart, and Jack Smart. Thanks to my climbing partners who are with me through thick and thin, fun and not so fun times, but always willing to hold the rope for another go at a route or just life in general. Also to all my friends at Group Publishing, especially Thom and Joani who have never waivered in their support of my family and me.

Thanks also have to go to my parents who guided me when I was younger. I'm sure you were wondering just what the boy would do in life; hopefully this gives you a good window. I can't thank you enough for the support. Also, my brother and sister who dropped everything and came to my side to help Cyn and the kids. Again, I can never thank you enough. Nor can I forget the small army of people who rescued me that horrible day on the mountain in Estes Park, starting with Steve Gorham and continuing on to the park rangers and the Larimer County search and rescue team: Matt Wilber, John Beh, Reggie Hughes, Doug Ridley, Bill Alexander, Mark Magnuson, Mark Ronca, Dan Ostrowski, and Bill Brown. I'm here today because of them.

But the biggest part of me that people don't get to see is my family. Mayah and Will, thank you both for giving me perspective and joy in my life. And to Cyndy, who I can never repay, other than to say and show that I love you more every day. You are an amazing person, friend, lover, and my biggest supporter. Thank you.

1

FREEFALL

I remember that climbing anchor perfectly.

It was a hundred feet up on Sundance Buttress, offering relative safety and security through a jumble of bright yellow webbing and nylon cord held into the rock with three bolts. Each bolt had a coil of webbing with a ring on it, and I will never forget the vision of that yellow webbing, stark against the blue sky, as it shot away from me.

There was no slow motion, no crazy moment of weightlessness. I accelerated from zero to sixty in an instant. The anchor was moving up and away from me so fast that it became a bright yellow dot before I could blink.

I remember thinking, *Wow, there's a lot of slack in the line.* I wondered if Steve, my climbing partner, had been pulled off his feet when I'd leaned back into my climbing harness and let go of the cliff. I really expected the rope to snap tight at any second.

My body took control, somehow knowing my mind wasn't ready to come to grips with the horror of what was happening. My legs kicked out and pushed me away from the wall. As they did, I either turned to my side or simply turned my head to see where I was going. That's when the photographer in me came out. The trees and hillside came into focus with indescribable clarity. I actually noticed the way ponderosa pines have a kind of sag in them. I noticed how green they were, and how that contrasted with the colors of the hillside as it slanted away. My mind just locked on to that, desperately trying to protect me from realizing I was in free fall, and I wasn't stopping.

Steve and I had been working a route up Sundance called Whiteman, in Rocky Mountain National Park. Sundance is basically a giant, 1,000-foot-high egg on the westernmost end of Lumpy Ridge, and almost any climber will tell you there's not a pebble on it that's not worth climbing. Thus, it's no surprise there are more than a dozen recognized routes up it.

I'd never even heard of Whiteman before that day; it wasn't part of the original plan. The original plan, conceived a week earlier, had been to go up a different route called Turnkorner. It's a challenging climb, rated a 5.10b on the Yosemite Decimal System. To put that in perspective, a climb up a small pile of rocks would be something like a 5.1. As climbs get more vertical, handholds get smaller and farther between, and as the effort required gets higher, the Yosemite rating goes up. A 5.9 climb would probably be the extent of a recreational climb. As you get into 5.10, 5.11, and 5.12 routes, that's where you'll find only the most experienced climbers.

Steve had tried Turnkorner once before and, in his words, he'd gotten pretty beat up on it, so he was anxious to try it again. He had been climbing for seventeen years when we first met. I'd been at it for thirteen, and I knew I could handle a climb of that rating, despite the fact that I had felt sort of "off" all morning

I'd woken up with that feeling. Being a self-proclaimed Christian, you'd think I'd have taken a moment right there in bed to pray about the day ahead, but like most other days when everything was generally A-OK, God was far from my thoughts. I just chalked the weird vibe up to the usual excited/nervous feeling I always got before a climb. It wasn't any kind of sense of dread or foreboding; I just never could stand the waiting and anticipation that came before a climb. On the one hand, the more time there was to think about a climb the more time there was to start wondering what might go wrong. On the other, I was like a junkie and I needed to get my climbing fix. The more I had to wait, the more I'd turn into a rodeo bull trapped in a loading chute.

Usually, the second I started climbing that would all go away. I'd get completely focused on unraveling the complexities of each climb. In every other sport I'd done before, I could daydream about ten different things, but in climbing I was always hyper-focused. That left no room for worries about pressures at work, home, or school or any of the other concerns of day-to-day life; they were all swept away and I could focus on just tackling the next few feet of rock in front of me.

For a kid who grew up afraid of heights, a passion for mountain-eering doesn't make much sense, but that raw simplicity brought an undeniable sense of clarity. From the very first moment I experienced it, I was hooked. So it's no surprise then, as I waited for Steve to pick me up on the morning of July 21, that feeling of being off was gnawing at me.

To get my mind off it, I sought comfort in the little things. I was in my kitchen, serving my three-year-old daughter, Mayah, her one-millionth bowl of Cheerios in life. The weather was clear; that portended a good day of climbing. A photographer's mind, like that of anyone in the creative fields, never stops working and as I looked out the window a small part of me did notice again just how different the environment of Colorado is compared to what I grew up in back east. Even the light is different. We call it the "Alpine glow," and every day I notice the way it makes the mountains take shape, and how it works with the geometry of even the smallest rocks, giving each one its own unique shape and color. I can understand how easy it is for so many people to consider the natural world their "church," and how God might speak to us through the natural wonder all around us, but I had far too much else on my mind that morning to appreciate it.

I checked on my wife, Cyndy, who was moving a little more slowly than usual. She'd run a 50K the day before and she was, in a word, wrecked. Our one-year-old, Will, was fussing, so I kept the engine in "dad gear" until Steve rang the doorbell at 8:00.

It was a forty-five-minute drive to the park, then a two-plus-mile hike in to Sundance Buttress and the Turnkorner route. It's a nice winding hike through the forest, full of all that natural wonder, but it's also a bit deceptive. The trees grow close enough to form a canopy that blocks out the view, offering only fleeting glimpses of what's up ahead. It's almost like being on a ship in the fog, heading toward the shore. You know the rocks are out there, but you don't know where. You can't even see how big Sundance is until all of a sudden you come out from the canopy and there it is, all full of shock and awe, shooting right out of the ground at your feet and into the sky.

Steve and I talked most of the way along the trail, generally about his job, but that weird feeling stayed with me, and this time it didn't go away when I started climbing. I was loaded up with fifteen pounds of gear and none of it felt good. I was working harder than I thought I should and the sweat was making me cold. Even at the top of the first pitch I was still tense and unable to relax. I didn't say anything to Steve; I didn't want him to think I was anything other than solid, so I told myself to chill out and press on.

Steve led up to the second pitch, and we got to the same spot where he'd gotten worked the last time. Right then it started getting really windy, and at that point I was thinking that I just needed a good—or even mediocre—excuse to get out of this. That's when it started to rain.

When granite gets wet it turns into an ice rink, so we knew our climb was in jeopardy, but opted to wait a few minutes. Summer storms in the Rockies are notorious for coming in fast and disappearing like a guy who owes a debt, but this one was an exception. As the rain turned into a downpour, and then into hail, I had all the excuse I needed.

We made it to the ground thirty minutes later, cold and wet, but by then the rain and hail had stopped. More than stopped actually, the whole storm had pretty much vanished. The sky had gone from dark and miserable to beautiful blue, frosted with thick white clouds. The route was shot; it was almost entirely exposed to the elements, but that's when Steve mentioned Whiteman.

Steve had climbed it before. He knew enough about it to think it had been sheltered from the weather and might still be climbable. It's a 5.11 climb, about the limit of what I could walk up to and climb on sight. If I had known all along I'd be climbing it that day I'd have been nervous for sure. As Steve was describing it to me though, something about the challenge coupled with not being able to finish Turnkorner, despite my own desire to get off of it, led me to believe it would be a good climb both mentally and physically. We decided to at least give it a look and see if Steve was right about it being out of the weather.

We were staring up at it a few minutes later. It was bone dry.

The route starts out on a slab, a piece of rock that's not quite vertical, but slopes up at about a 60-degree angle. At the top of the slab the really meaty part of the climb starts; scattered small cracks and "credit card handholds" separated by a series of completely smooth sections. About 100 feet up there's a small ledge with a pre-placed anchor bolted into the rock.

I tied in to my harness and made my way to the top of the slab, where I looked around for a spot where I could set my first piece of hardware. I was carrying a rack of about nine or ten cams and a full spectrum of nuts—pieces of shaped metal or aluminum, all of which are designed to protect climbers in case of a fall. Basically, you set a cam or a nut into a crack, slip your rope into it, and it becomes a safety anchor. The more you climb, the more creative you get about finding places to set your gear, but there's nothing like setting that first piece on a tough climb. It's an instant confidence booster.

I set my first nut and called down to Steve that I was "on belay." Typically in climbing, while one person is making his way up the rock his climbing harness is tethered to his partner, who has fed the rope through a belay device on his own harness. If the climber falls, the belayer, who never takes his hands off the rope, drops his hand to his waist, effectively applying a brake to the climber's fall. The climber can then be lowered to the ground, or grab the wall and try again.

Steve shouted up some encouragement and I continued on, finally shedding that weird feeling that had been nagging at me, and really getting into the climb. Usually I tend to muscle my way through climbs, but Whiteman wasn't going to let me do that. It's a very precise and technical route that requires planning ahead for each calculated sequence of moves to advance. Instead of climbing the whole thing in my head first, I literally had to plan it foot by foot.

I'd made it about three quarters of the way to the small ledge when I got to a huge blank section. I stopped and looked around, trying to figure out the puzzle, and saw a good handhold a little ways off. I knew if I could make it to that handhold I'd be in the money. The path to the ledge from that point was pretty clear, but getting to the handhold was going to require three or four body moves across that blank space.

I had about 90 feet of rope out behind me at this point, and was feeling a little exposed as I started making my way across. I had to move very slowly. The handholds I could find were ridiculously small, "dime edges" as they say in climbing parlance—and in that whole section I was simultaneously pushing up with my feet and pushing down with my hands. That kind of climbing is what makes Whiteman particularly devious. You can't move too fast or you'll end up spinning yourself right off the rock, but if you go too slow, you'll get tired and just fall off.

I should say here that falling is part of climbing and, strange as it sounds, the more you climb the more you fall. The difference that comes with experience is you learn to fall safely so you don't crash into anything, like outcroppings or other climbers, before the rope snaps tight and stops you. By the time Steve and I approached the base of Whiteman that day, we'd both experienced more than a hundred falls. We both understood that if you placed your gear right and tied your rope right, falling is generally no big deal. You just curse under your breath and start over.

As I was making my way through that blank spot, eyeing the handhold, the fear of getting hurt had little to do with me not wanting to fall. I just didn't want to blow it.

The sequence I'd planned was perfect, and just twenty minutes after I'd left Steve, I was a hundred feet up, letting out a victory yell and clipping into the anchor. Even now I can remember how good that webbing felt as I grabbed on to it and clipped in.

I shouted down to Steve that I was "off belay," meaning that I was safe. Hearing this, he unhooked from the rope and went to his pack to put on his climbing shoes.

That was where the exuberance of a successful climb, that weird "off" feeling, and too much confidence caught up with me. In my mind, the plan was for Steve to lower me to the ground and then take his turn on the climb. As he was getting his shoes ready, I was preparing to release from the anchor so I could get down.

> I've thought a lot about the simple and tiny little things I could have done differently at that moment.

The problem was, we hadn't really discussed the plan. Steve was putting his shoes on thinking he was going to join me on the ledge, 100 feet up.

I checked my knot and yelled down, "Okay, it's all you!"

Steve thought I was ready to bring him up and shouted "okay" back up to me.

I've thought a lot about the simple and tiny little things I could have done differently at that moment. I could have shouted "on belay," the universal announcement climbers make when they're ready to begin, which must be followed by the partner shouting "belay on" to announce it's okay to start climbing. Every six-year-old who goes to a birthday party at their neighborhood climbing gym learns to do that. I could have turned and looked behind me, and I'd have seen Steve wasn't hooked in, and we could have had an interesting conversation right there about just what we each were thinking.

Instead, at that moment, I made the mistake of being too complacent. When Steve shouted "okay" up to me, I let go of the anchor and leaned back from the wall.

From what Steve has told me, I fell horizontally, which is unusual. The human body is essentially top heavy, and when people fall more than a few feet they tend to go into a headfirst position that, no question, would have killed me. There was still a rope in my harness, and while it wasn't slowing me down in the least, it was somehow providing just enough resistance to keep me horizontal . . . not that hitting the ground that way would have been much better. It's a pretty well accepted fact that if you hit the ground like you're lying down, you're dead. The only real chance of surviving a fall of that height is to land on your feet.

God obviously knew that, which is why he put a gnarled, rugged, burned-out tree right in my path. I don't remember hitting it. No one in their right mind would ever think to even aim for it, but I slammed into one of the branches with my head at full speed, and at just the perfect angle to pivot me into a standing position as I went down.

I don't remember hitting the ground, but I know I landed feetfirst. That was when my ankles exploded.

I didn't black out. One second I was falling and the next I was aware that I was lying on my back somewhere in a small field of dishwasher-sized boulders, looking up at the rock wall I'd just been climbing. I was at the base of the slab, almost in the exact spot I'd started from. Shock set in and robbed me of my memory. There was no yellow anchor webbing, or blue sky, or green aspens. Only confusion.

I shouldn't be here.

That was my first thought. My second was that I really, really needed the pain to stop.

Pain. *I shouldn't be here.* Pain. *I shouldn't be here.* It was as if my mind was still trying to catch up and understand what had just happened. I couldn't possibly be lying on the ground; I was still supposed to be a hundred feet up, planning my next move.

Steve was screaming. That's what I was aware of next. He was screaming my name at the top of his lungs and running toward me. I started to ask what he was yelling about, but at that same instant I felt an almost blinding pain in my back. The closest thing I can think of is it felt like I had a rock shoved into my back, stabbing me. I'd never felt that kind of pain. So intense. It was all I could think about, and I just wanted it to stop.

When Steve got to me he was still yelling, asking if I was alive and if I could hear him. I looked into his eyes and all I saw was complete terror. I couldn't move, so I couldn't see all the blood on the ground or what my body looked like. Just the fear in Steve's eyes—he was crying—and the pain coming in waves so intense I couldn't speak until each wave passed.

I kept asking Steve what happened. I don't know if he answered me or how many times I asked, but eventually I told him there was a rock in my back and I needed him to please move me off it.

As I picture the scene, I can see Steve looking down at me, certain I've got either a broken back, broken neck, or both, and knowing that moving me is absolutely the worst thing he could do.

He did it anyway.

Maybe he thought he couldn't possibly hurt me any worse at that point. He was probably doing the math in his head: the basic rule is that if you fall 10 feet you have a 10 percent chance of dying, a 20 percent chance at 20 feet, 30 at 30 and so on. I'd fallen 100 feet. Maybe he thought making me comfortable was about the only thing anyone was going to be able to do for me. All I knew was that the pain just had to stop. It hurt so much I was almost hyperventilating.

Steve grabbed me under my arm and dragged me off the boulder onto a flat spot on the dirt about ten feet away and put a pack under my head. And I *did* feel better. Somehow, just being in a different spot, away from where I'd landed, made a difference.

Steve started doing the best he could to stop the bleeding and apply first aid. He wrapped a piece of webbing around my leg in a tourniquet, which seemed to work, and I think that helped him get focused. He covered me with some of the loose clothing from the pack to try to keep me warm. I remember being a little amazed at how calm and in control he was as he was trying to talk to me about a plan. We were still two and a half miles from my truck.

I was deep in shock by then and trying to stay awake as Steve was talking about how he needed to leave me there, alone, so he could run back to the truck and get help. He guessed it would take forty-five minutes to get to the truck, ten more minutes to drive into the town of Estes Park and get help, and then who-knew-how-long before I could be found again. I don't think he had any hope of finding me alive when he got back, but he did his best to encourage me, promising me he would run faster than he ever had in his life. I told him I'd be there when he got back.

I wasn't trying to be funny or brave; I was already too out of it for that. The truth was I was terrified at being left there. I was already so cold and all I could think about was how cold I would be.

Steve took off at a full sprint, but in less than a minute he was back above me, shouting again.

"I have my phone! I have my phone!" he was saying as he rummaged through the pack under my head.

I was fading back into the fog. I didn't know why he was back so soon and shouting. I almost wanted to ask why he wasn't at the car. He never, ever brought his phone with him when he went climbing. He had a job in sales, selling yellow page ads, and the last thing he wanted to do on his time off was talk on the phone. There was also no point. Wherever he went climbing, there was never any coverage. Today, of all days, his wife had asked him to bring it, and he'd broken with tradition. He pulled the phone out of his pack and turned it on.

Keep in mind, we were at the base of a 1,000-foot buttress, two miles from the nearest road, and in the middle of the national park wilderness.

Steve dialed 911.

And somebody answered.

2

A SERIES OF MIRACLES

By my count, it took eight miracles for me to survive the fall and get to the hospital alive. The first was that according to the Park Service's investigation, the various pieces of protection that my rope had been looped through had caused some friction on the rope and had likely decreased both the velocity of my fall and the force of my body hitting the ground.

The second was hitting the tree on the way down, slowing me even further, and pivoting my feet toward the ground. The third was Steve bringing his phone. The fourth was that it actually worked.

I don't know what would have happened if he had been one foot to the left or right of where he was when he pressed the send button. More than likely there would have been no signal and Steve would have had no choice but to leave me there, broken, cold, and dying.

Had he left me, I'm certain I would have fallen asleep, bled out, and just slipped away. Instead, somehow, he was inside a cone of reception and the operator was on the line instantly.

Steve spoke loud and fast. I don't remember all the words he said—my perception of the world was only coming in through short windows of clarity—but I've read and heard the 911 transcript since then, and to this day it still chills me.

Steve pleaded for rangers to come to the base of Whiteman right away, and the operator didn't waste any time. She told him to stay right where he was so he wouldn't lose the signal, and patched him in to the Rocky Mountain National Park rangers. Steve told them everything he could about what had happened and where we were.

I was fading in and out of reality, but in one of my clearer moments I remember Steve was back by my side, looking at me.

"They're coming," he said. "Help is coming."

Just knowing he wasn't going to leave me, that I wasn't going to be trapped all alone in a terrifying world of silence and pain with no end in sight, covered me with a sense of relief that was even more comforting than the news that rescue was on the way.

He looked in my eyes and asked if I wanted him to call Cyndy. I had no idea how bad I really was. I couldn't see my legs or the blood, and other than the pain in my back I couldn't feel much else. I had no information to give her and I didn't want her to worry. I told Steve no, and he didn't fight me. He went right back to work doing what he could to slow the bleeding.

He was also talking incessantly. In my deranged state I never gave a thought to the effort he was making just to try to keep me awake and focused. In a funny way it worked because, as bad as it sounds, I started getting annoyed. My body and mind were trying to shut down, but he kept jabbering on so much, constantly pulling me back out of the fog, and I wanted to scream at him to just shut up.

I once heard an ambulance driver in a movie talking about the difference between the ones who survive the ride to the hospital and the ones who don't. In his words, the ones who kept their eyes open were the ones who made it. There's no question in my mind that Steve saved my life in several ways that day. Keeping me awake was one of them.

The next two miracles involved Gabriel.

Eric Gabriel was taking his lunch break when Steve's 911 call came in. He was on duty as a ranger and a park medic, covering a patrol area that could have easily placed him more than an hour away from me. As God would have it, however, Eric decided to have lunch at home that day, only a few miles from Lumpy Ridge. Of all the places on the map Eric's job could have placed him, when the call for help came he was already at the closest possible point. Miracle five.

He also knew exactly where we were. Being a climber himself, he knew all the routes up Sundance, and was particularly familiar with Whiteman. The previous summer there had been an accident with another climber in almost the same spot. Eric knew not only how to get there but also how to run a rescue operation to get an accident victim out of there along the fastest possible route. Miracle number six.

In only took Eric forty minutes from the instant the call came in to gear up, drive out, and run in to where I was lying. To me, it seemed like he was there instantly, but for him, he later confided, it was a long trek to what he thought would be the scene of a fatality.

Steve once described the vision of Eric coming into view around the corner as being like an angel arriving. With a name like Gabriel, of course, that makes perfect sense.

I didn't see him at first. All I heard was him shouting, "Craig, can you hear me?"

He was surprised to find me not only alive but alert. As he knelt over me, his first words to me are impossible to forget.

"Okay, Craig, we're here," he said. "We're going to get you out of here."

I liked him immediately.

Just like his namesake, Eric Gabriel became for me God's strength, although I confess putting it in those terms is the result of years of after-the-fact reflection. On that day, Eric was just a strong and calming presence that had little to do with God and everything to do with the fact I could tell he knew exactly what to do to get me out of there.

I was still feeling cold and weak, and the pain was still gripping me in waves. I was getting nauseous. As Eric got right to work I was pretty well out of it and there was a lot that he made sure not to tell me. It was only through later conversations that I learned about everything he thought, said, and did that day.

He first noticed that bones were sticking out of both my legs at the ankles. I was bleeding and in obvious pain, but beyond that there was no way he could know what was wrong with me. He was absolutely astounded that I had no head injuries. Even he later called that *miraculous*.

He got an IV started and set about stopping the bleeding in my legs. He didn't bother trying to reset the bones. My guess is they were so shattered that he saw no point in it and just went about wrapping them up as best he could. What concerned him was what he couldn't see, things like internal bleeding and other invisible horrors that could creep up and kill me, silently and suddenly. I wasn't showing any obvious signs of that, but Eric knew he was fighting against a clock. My body would only be able to supply oxygen to itself for so long.

I'd had a traumatic injury, which carried a huge risk of sudden blood loss that would lead to hypovolemic shock. Without enough blood volume, my heart wouldn't be able to get enough blood to my other organs and one by one they would begin to fail. The IV he put in would help maintain the volume of liquid in my system, but it could only be a temporary fix. He could stop the external bleeding, but he had no way of knowing whether or how much I was bleeding internally and it was easy to assume the worst. I was losing blood like sand running through an hourglass, and when enough sand ran out, it'd be game over.

I also had a severe central nervous system injury, which created the added risk of neurogenic shock. Something in my body was telling all of my blood vessels to dilate instead of constrict to restrict blood flow. When all the blood vessels dilate at once, there's not enough blood to go around. Instead, the blood just pools away from the heart, the organs don't get enough oxygen, and shock sets in.

I was already bleeding out from my injuries, and my own body was making things worse. With every passing minute, Eric faced a greater risk of losing me.

But holding death at bay was only half his job.

Fortunately, only a handful of people need first aid and rescue in the wilderness each year, but the downside is that it's only those few people who get a true understanding and appreciation for the incredible skill people like Eric bring to an emergency. In a car accident on the freeway, for example, you'll have police, fire department, and paramedics all on the scene in a matter of minutes. In the first few minutes Eric was with me, all alone, he was splitting the duty of saving my life on the spot—equipped with little more than a stethoscope, IVs, and bandages—and coordinating the rescue operation that was going to get me to a hospital. He spoke to me, asked me questions and encouraged me, while simultaneously treating my injuries, stabilizing me as best he could, and coordinating the logistics of rallying all the rescue gear and personnel needed to lower me to the valley floor, and to have a helicopter waiting.

There was no question they were going to have to carry me out. The Park Service was not equipped with a "short haul" system, whereby they could have lowered a cable to a basket and flown me out to a clearing where they could have set me down, landed the helicopter, and loaded me in. Even if they had been, the altitude and unpredictable winds would have made such an operation incredibly dangerous, and not just for me.

As he was stabilizing me, Eric asked if I wanted to call my wife and, as I had with Steve earlier, I said no. I didn't know if everything was going to be all right yet, and until I did, calling her would only make her worry.

When I had stood at my own kitchen window earlier that morning, I'd smelled the smoke of far-off fires burning. The Big Elk Meadows fire was burning between Estes Park and Lyons. That was the year the governor had gone on TV and said the whole state was burning. At the time I had let the smoky aroma carry me back to my childhood days, when my parents would burn leaves in the yard and the cold crisp air would mingle with the smell of smoke, signaling that fall was ending and winter was coming. I gave no thought at the time to how such a huge fire could hamper a rescue effort. Already, the Big Elk Fire had killed three people, two in a tanker and one in a helicopter crash.

Eric needed fifteen to twenty people to get me safely off the mountain. At almost any other time—even without the fires—such a team would have to be gathered from all the points of the compass, possibly over a matter of hours. A major fire emergency could have made it even longer, but on that day a whole crew arrived on scene, including several volunteers from Larimer County search and rescue, in only forty-five minutes. Miracle number seven.

The second rescuer on the scene was Matt Wilber. He arrived only a couple of minutes after Eric, and Eric was very glad to see him. Matt was also an experienced ranger and climber. He and Eric had worked together on the rescue that previous August, equipping him also with the knowledge of how to get me out of there in the fastest possible way. With him to coordinate the evacuation, Eric was free to focus more exclusively on caring for me.

They had to "package" me up to get me out. I was still on a large pile of big, loose stones, covered with logs, sticks, and pine needles. Just walking was difficult, and trying to carry an injured climber out of there by hand would be almost impossible. They couldn't just put me on a stretcher and carry me out of there; it would be too easy for someone to slip and send the stretcher crashing down the hillside with parts of me spilling out of it. They had to make sure I was completely immobilized and then, through a series of ropes and pulleys, they were going to have to slowly and painstakingly lower me more than 1,000 vertical feet to level ground.

Eric and Matt made sure the equipment they needed to get me down arrived first, so I could be packaged and ready by the time the whole team arrived. They had to roll me onto a backboard first. They tried to be as gentle as they could, but it was still one of the worst parts of my day.

They put a mask on me to try to keep oxygen flowing into my system and stave off shock. To secure me to the backboard they had to tie my arms down. I was doing okay with it until they put the shield over me.

Standard procedure for a trauma victim at the base of a cliff is to place a clear Plexiglas shield over their face. No one could know if some loose stone was going to come tumbling down the cliff face and smack me. The shield was for my protection, but it sent me over the edge of reason and I freaked out.

With the mask on and my arms tied, I couldn't move. I was also in a C-collar to keep my neck and spine immobile, and when they put that shield over me I suddenly felt completely confined and smothered. Even with the oxygen, I felt like I couldn't breathe. My back was killing me. I started to hyperventilate.

Before I was done, I was shouting at them to please, *please* take the shield off, thinking somehow that'd help me breathe better. It was only after I really began to voice my opinion that they took it off. The rescue operation went on at full tilt, but as much as they could, they let me be.

I kept rotating from pain to fear to hope to frustration. I didn't know why they weren't just fixing me. I don't know how many times I asked about getting something to deal with the pain, but the answer always came back no, they weren't sure it'd be safe. I found out later it was because they suspected my right lung had collapsed. What little blood I had left to carry oxygen to the rest of my body was getting that much less oxygen from my lungs. Pain meds would only depress my breathing even more, and without the trauma equipment on hand to mitigate the risk that I would simply stop breathing, there was nothing they could do.

When they were ready, they put me into a "bean bag" body vacuum splint, which conforms to the body and keeps the person in it warm. It makes for a good cocoon and prevents a lot of the bumping and jostling that comes with being carried in a litter. It doesn't prevent all of it, however, and Eric made sure I knew that.

"It's going to hurt when we move you," he said. "I still can't give you any pain meds, so instead I'm going to ask you to focus on that pain. Right now your survival is as much up to you as it is to me. I'm going to fight as hard as I can and I need you to fight just as hard. I need you to focus on that pain, control it, and put it into a compartment somewhere in your mind where you can deal with it as we go along."

It was quite a speech, but despite it, Eric really didn't know if I was going to live long enough to see the helicopter. The whole time, he told me what he was doing but didn't tell me anything about how badly I was hurt or what he was concerned might be wrong with me. I'm glad for that. Had he told me everything, I just don't know how I would have reacted. Maybe I'd have been calm about it, or maybe I'd have started to panic. Instead, being able to just focus on the pain in my back gave me only one thing to be concerned about, one thing I could believe I would overcome, instead of trying to deal with everything at once.

That's really the way people endure any situation. They focus on one thing at a time and deal with the small pieces of their problem individually; then, over time, the pieces come together to form the bigger picture. That's why I usually disagree with the popular belief that "God doesn't give you more than you can handle." It's not that simple. God gives you the tools you need in order to deal with what you have to endure right now, and you don't need to face the whole big picture all at once. You focus on the little pieces and have the faith to know that you can endure those and then move on to the next thing. Over time the pieces all come together, and later on you can see how God worked in every moment of your life. Knowing what I know now, I can say with certainty that my rescue and evacuation were no exception.

I shudder at the truth of it, but God was the furthest thing from my mind.

I wish I could say that those thoughts were on my mind that day. I shudder at the truth of it, but God was the furthest thing from my mind. Granted I was not exactly in top form—my thought patterns could hardly be called linear that day—but the old saying that you really find out who you are in a crisis is true. There was no thought of asking God for help or thanking Him that I was alive. When I was in the moment, my thoughts were only on the pain, the frustration that they couldn't make it go away, and trying to know what was happening.

To the latter point, even though no one was telling me anything overtly, Eric did something that really clued me in to how bad things were. For a second time, he asked me if I wanted to call my wife.

He did it very casually, along the lines of "We're going to get you out of here, but hey, why don't we give Cyndy a call?"

They had started to move me and I was in la-la land, watching the trees and the clouds slowly move along overhead and thinking it was strangely nice, but when Eric asked about Cyndy again, it brought on another moment of clarity. At first I just thought it was a strange question, why would he care so much about me calling Cyndy?

My first gut reaction was to say no again, but it nagged at me that Eric thought calling her might be important. I began to wonder if I was hurt much worse than I'd thought. I was feeling cold and confused. They weren't giving me any pain medicine. They weren't fixing me. Something clicked in my brain and I thought yes, I did want to call her. I wanted to see her. I knew if I could see her it would calm me. Seeing her would make me feel better. I told him yes.

It was Steve who made the call. He was off a little distance from me and I couldn't hear everything, but Cyndy filled me in later on what was said.

She was a little surprised to hear him on the other end of the line, but figured it was just a heads-up and asked if we were on our way home.

"No," Steve said. "There's been an accident. Craig fell and broke his ankles. But he's going to be okay."

All Cyndy really got from the call was that I'd taken a big fall and gotten hurt, but she didn't know how bad and didn't even know I'd fallen and actually hit the ground. Their conversation was short; Steve simply said he had to go and that was all.

The next thing I knew, Cyndy was looking down at me. She'd called Steve's wife, Lisa, and the two of them had driven out to the park to see for themselves what was going on. It didn't occur to me then that after they parked, she had to make the two-mile trek to where I was on legs that had just hammered out a 50K run less than twenty-four hours earlier.

Sore as she was that morning when I'd left, the adrenaline took over and she did what she had to do to get to me. She and Lisa ran the whole way in.

What I saw in her eyes was the worst, even though she was smiling. When she worries she gets a little furrow in her brow. I saw that times ten. She'd spoken with Eric first when she'd caught up to us, and he'd tried to prepare her for what she was going to see. It was starting to dawn on her that this involved a lot more than broken ankles.

The first two things I told here were that I loved her and that I was sorry. I'm not sure what order I used.

She told me the two things she knew I needed to hear. She loved me and the kids were fine.

I thought about how amazing she was. To look at me and know what I needed to hear, and to tell me she loved me even though I was a train wreck, was just amazing. And then she was gone, stepping out of the way so Eric and his crew could do their jobs.

Once they started to move me, it took my rescuers more than an hour to get me down the mountain. It seemed like forever. It sounded like there were twenty people all around, every one of them hollering. I couldn't see any of it. My world was pine trees and the occasional patch of sky. The rest was a confused sense of chaos.

They used two 300-foot ropes and a lot of sweat to move me, inch by inch, for more than a mile. It was a very slow, very involved and deliberate process, all designed to provide a very controlled and stabilized descent. Two guys would run ahead and set up anchors on a couple of trees, one guy would stay behind on a radio, everyone else was with me. The rope was tied to the litter and the guy on the radio would supply slack or tension through a sort of belay device based on commands from the operation leader.

When they reached the end of one 300-foot rope, they reset everything with the second rope and did it over again, and over again, leapfrogging me all the way down. Every few minutes Eric would appear, encouraging me, telling me to deal with the pain, asking me to hang in there, yelling at me to stay awake.

Then, after five leapfrogs, suddenly everything started moving much faster.

They'd finally gotten me down to the trail, where they could lower a wheel on the litter and literally run me to where the helicopter was waiting.

The fact that the helicopter was there might not seem like a full-fledged miracle (number eight that day), until you consider how many things could have prevented it. Any helicopter pilot who's spent time in the area can tell you that weather, wind conditions, and even the air density at that altitude are a crapshoot, even on the best days. With the storms that had rolled through earlier in the day, it's possible the helicopter could have been grounded, but the storms had all moved off to the east, and the forecast from the National Weather Service was enough to green-light an airlift. Or the fire operations might have made the helicopter unavailable. It was also getting dark. In another hour or so, there wouldn't have been enough light to airlift me. Had it not been for the rescue operation the previous August charting the course for my evacuation, the slow and deliberate process of getting me off the mountain could have taken twice as long and I would have missed my ride.

Glad as I am for the speed of my rescue though, the sad truth is that the climber they tried to rescue back in August died in the hospital. His name was Tim DeBeau. He was forty-four years old.

They set me on the ground and did some final checking, and somehow in that moment I had the presence of mind to tell the guys that my car keys were in my pocket and to give them to Cyndy. They did, but no doubt they were as puzzled as I am to this day about how or why I thought of that, but it spared Cyndy from having to make another trip up to get the car. Small blessings are still blessings.

Up to that point my rescuers had been perfect. I was hurting a lot, but all things considered, they'd managed to get a 200-pound champagne glass off the mountain without so much as nicking it. They were all glad to see the helicopter, and they all knew the importance of every single second. Tired as they all were, I can imagine them running all the faster as the helicopter came into view and the flight nurse opened the door. That's why it's easy for me to understand how, as they lifted me off the ground and loaded me onto the helicopter, they slammed my feet into the bulkhead and bent them backwards, shattered bone and all.

For the first time that day, I screamed.

I thought I'd experienced pain at its worst, but in that last moment it went to a level beyond anything I could have imagined. And it was escalating.

The flight nurse was on me in an instant.

"Okay, I'm going to give you something for the pain," he said. He was right over my face, jabbing a needle into the IV line. His face and that needle are the last thing I remember as I pitched headlong into oblivion. There was no light. There was no sound. I've read all these books where people talk about hearing voices and talking to God, but for me there was none of that. There was no pain. There was no wife, no kids, no God. As much as I might have wanted those things to be there, there was nothing. It was only blackness.

Had I thought to pray at all that day, or noticed even one of the miracles that had happened, it might have been different.

3

AWAKE AND SCARED

I woke up in ICU two days later.

To me no time had passed, but for all those around me, whether they were family and friends who spent every minute wondering if my life was ebbing away, or doctors and hospital staff fighting tirelessly to keep me alive, each passing moment was a marathon.

Everything that would determine whether I lived or died happened in those forty-eight hours, and from the moment the helicopter landed, it didn't look good. I had too much stacked against me. I had lost a lot of blood, I had several broken bones, it had taken hours to get me to a trauma center, and I was facing a huge infection risk from the dirt and debris that had gotten into my legs.

It's easy to imagine the doctors wondering where to start. Or even if they should. From the moment they first saw me, they'd given me only one hour to live.

As bad as things looked for me, those were the worst two days of Cyndy's life.

Back in the park, after the evac team got me loaded and the helicopter took off, Eric went straight to Cyndy.

"Hey," he said. "Take some deep breaths. You don't need to rush to get to him. Take your time, drive *safely* and expect that they're going to be very busy with him when you get there."

Cyndy asked where the helicopter was taking me. The closest trauma center was Poudre Valley Hospital in Fort Collins. It was already getting dark as she and Lisa jogged two miles back to the car and started the hour-plus drive to the hospital. Steve followed behind in my truck. Most of the ride was spent in silence until, about twenty minutes outside Fort Collins, Cyndy called the hospital.

They were very eager to talk to her.

Within seconds she was speaking to Dr. Don Turner, a neurosurgeon who'd already finished his shift, but had stayed on when the call came in. Instead of being at home with his family, he'd spent the last half hour trying to find someone who could give him the consent he needed to operate on me.

They had me on a ventilator to keep me breathing and to keep the oxygen in my system, and had run a few MRIs to try to figure out where to devote their attention first. They had a battle plan, but until they got consent there wasn't much more they could do.

Cyndy still had no idea about the severity of my condition. Her frame of reference was still limited to broken ankles, but the fact that the hospital staff was relieved to hear from her, and the fact that there was a neurosurgeon on the other end of the line, suddenly made it clear that things were more serious than she first thought.

Her response to the consent request, like Cyndy herself, was direct. "Yes! Of course!"

She tried asking for more information, but there was a lot Dr. Turner didn't know yet. His voice and his tone were both very grim. He couldn't take time to give Cyndy any details, but he did give her a word of advice.

"I think you should call Craig's parents."

With that, he had to get off the phone and get back to seeing what he could do to save me.

Cyndy spent the next few minutes slightly stunned, but she made the call, still not fully understanding my condition. By the time she arrived at the hospital, I'd already been in surgery about twenty minutes, and there was a grief counselor waiting to talk with her. She thought that was a little odd. She wasn't grieving. Not yet.

Given how little Cyndy knew at that point, comfort was not at all what she needed. Lisa was there, and all Cyndy really wanted was to know as much as she could about what was going on.

Steve joined them after a short while, and the waiting began. At one point, a few hours later, a nurse came out and told Cyndy what little she could. I was still in surgery, but I'd been coherent and speaking when I'd arrived at the hospital. I'd known my middle name, the date, and a few other bits of trivia. That was encouraging news, but that was the only news she had.

As the hours wore on, the silence and the darkness outside became easier to deal with than running through all the what-ifs. The grief counselor had left hours before, seeming to understand that Cyndy was okay for the moment. Cyndy herself had run out of things to talk about with Lisa and Steve, and was praying silently. Praying for answers. Praying for our future. Praying that everything would be okay.

Well after midnight, Dr. Turner came out and sat down with Cyndy. The grim tone was still in his voice, and it had spread to his eyes.

For the first time, Cyndy learned the full extent of my injuries, inside and out. The list was too long to memorize, and ultimately it didn't matter. The most important news came last.

"He's come through the surgery. We'll just have to wait and see," was the best he could offer.

Seeing me at that point just wasn't an option, so Dr. Turner told her to go home and get a couple hours of sleep. It was the classic example of "there's nothing more you can do here, so go home and get some rest." No matter what happened, she would need her strength, and a little sleep would do her some good.

Not even Cyndy can remember all of what happened over the next several hours. Just as I had been fading in and out of reality right after the fall, Cyndy was struggling to understand what her new reality might be. While I'd been in physical shock, she was in mental and emotional shock, unaware of the passing of time or the little details of life going on all around her.

Steve drove her home, where her friend Audrey was waiting. Audrey, a mother and wife herself, had dropped everything on the day of the accident to watch our kids so Cyndy could be by my side. Audrey wasn't sure if she should stay or go, but Steve told her she really needed to stay, and she did.

Cyndy tried to get some sleep, but only managed to spend a lot of time crying, worrying through what had become a waking nightmare, and wondering how I could have done this to all of them.

As she left for the hospital again a few hours later, Audrey volunteered to stay on at the house. She stayed there, providing comfort and care to our kids, for three days. We should all have friends like her.

As Cyndy arrived back in the waiting room she met Dr. Douglas Lundy and, truth be told, she didn't much care for him. At least not at first.

Dr. Lundy is both a superb physician and a straight shooter who calls it like he sees it. The result is that he doesn't need to guess very often; he's a pretty accurate judge of a situation. What Cyndy initially mistook for arrogance she came to realize was in fact a confidence that comes with knowing how to read a medical situation and understanding what to do about it. Before long, she also realized that his confidence was what she, and I, really needed.

Dr. Lundy answered the most important question first. I was still alive, but he hadn't expected me to make it through the night.

That revelation was a sickening blow. Cyndy had known I was very seriously hurt but her mind had never even arrived at the idea that I might die. It was beyond comprehension. I couldn't die. That was not in her plan. That was not in *our* plan. Our kids needed me. We had dreams for our lives and our future together, and they could not suddenly be gone.

Dr. Lundy reassured her quickly. The fact that I had made it through the night also meant that I was likely out of the woods in terms of surviving the accident.

It also meant a whole list of different kinds of questions. Would I be paralyzed? Would I ever be able to walk again? What was life going to be like?

Of course no one could know those answers so early, but Dr. Lundy didn't waste any time raising false hope. He was pretty sure both my feet were going to have to come off—they were so blown apart it was hard to imagine anything else. Cyndy didn't argue; if it needed to be done then just do it, was her thinking. Nonetheless, he really wanted to try to save them, and for the moment there was no need to rush any decision on that.

He went back to work and Cyndy spent the day worrying, greeting friends, praying, pleading for answers, and waiting. I was in the ICU, where there were no windows, and nothing for Cyndy to look at but my wrecked and unconscious body. She became my advocate and my champion, a role she would continue to play for the next year and a half. All she needed me to do on that first day was just wake up.

The first thing I remember is someone's hands on my head. I'd been aware of nothing at all before then, but there was suddenly no question that someone was holding my head, and turning it.

As my eyes creaked open and I focused on a man who was looking at me, only one thought came to mind.

He looks just like Ricardo Montalban.

He was obviously a doctor, very dapper, with slicked back silver hair. As he looked at me, the drugs took over. I believed that he could read my mind, and that he knew all about the Montalban thing. I told myself that was crazy, and I had a whole argument with myself in my head about it.

As I kept coming to, he was talking to me, but I was having a hard time understanding the words. I felt like I was floating and it was like he was talking through syrup. He seemed to understand I was still coming around, or at least he perceived that I wasn't getting what he was saying, so he kept at it.

Eventually I figured out he was telling me that I was okay, but I'd been in a very bad accident. He told me I was in the hospital and that they were taking very good care of me. I could see the ventilator tube going down my mouth, breathing for me. He didn't tell me anything else about my injuries, not then.

While he was talking I was trying to remember everything that had happened, but I only had bits and pieces. I remembered that I'd fallen, but I didn't remember where I'd been when I fell or the carry out. I assumed I was in the hospital, but I didn't know that I'd hurt my back and I had no idea how bad my feet and ankles were hurt. All I knew for sure was that I couldn't feel anything at all below my legs. And I couldn't move.

My arms were restrained, partly to stop me from trying to sit up and partly to prevent me from any kind of thrashing around that would rip the tubes out of them. I was also wearing a C-collar, which is basically a big plastic and foam neck brace that juts up under your chin so you can't really see much past your own nose. I found myself suddenly living in a very, very small world: the collar, the ventilator tube, the ceiling, and the doctor standing over me. I couldn't even see my own chest.

I don't remember what else the doctor was saying or trying to say. I started to wonder if I was paralyzed, but fatigue overtook me and I fell back to sleep.

Those first couple days back in the world were like a series of short films, where I'd hear voices and open my eyes to see something going on around me, and then pass out again. I could only stay awake for a few minutes. I was socked deep in a medication fog, and life was little more than small windows of reality separated by long blank spaces.

Sometimes I'd wake up and see my parents. Other times it was friends. Most of the time it was just the nurses. One time I saw Cyndy. She was visibly upset. We couldn't talk to each other, not with the ventilator in, but we held hands as she cried. I couldn't help blaming myself for how upset she was. I think most men don't want to be seen as frail, weak, and having paid the price for something big. At that moment I was all three of those things. I felt the pain of messing things up, and forcing her to pay just as big a price as I was.

I woke up to the same nurse most of the time. I'd open my eyes and she'd be there, cleaning the tubes or doing some other work. She was always professional but also friendly and nice. It got to the point that I felt like we were bonding. I hadn't gotten much more information about my overall condition from the doctors, but I figured this nurse, who was apparently in the room with me constantly, probably had a good idea about what was really wrong with me.

By day three they'd given me a notepad and pen, and the restraints were off. I could move my arms and hands fine, so I'd write notes and people would answer me verbally. As I looked at the nurse and made eye contact, I didn't bother with the pen. I pointed to my feet and used my fingers to mime the act of walking. I looked back at her and let my eyes ask the rest of the question.

And then this friendly, nice, and professional nurse jerked me out of the medication fog and into stark reality. She started crying.

Up until that moment, I'd simply been assuming that I just needed to serve my time while my body healed and then one day I'd just spring off the bed and go home. In an instant, that vision was gone.

She tried to pull it together quickly, without much success.

"Your back is broken," she said, "and we're really not sure what's going to happen."

She said something else about the doctors doing everything they could and how they were all going to take the best care of me, but I wasn't hearing it. I barely even noticed that she left the room, leaving me alone in my tiny world with a fresh set of demons to torment me.

I couldn't breathe. She didn't tell me that the real issue for the moment wasn't whether I was going to walk. She didn't tell me the real issue was whether I was going to keep my legs.

In hindsight, I think that was best. I didn't realize it then, but her reaction prepared me for what would be a lot more bad news to come. It was a slap, yes, but it was also like letting just a little air out of the balloon instead of suddenly popping it. Once again, it was God giving me just enough to deal with.

The denial came on quickly. "This," whatever it was, was not what I needed now. I told myself it was ridiculous and that she couldn't be right. Whatever she was afraid of wasn't going to happen to *me*. Maybe to someone else, or to most regular people, but not me. How bad could it be if I wasn't writhing in pain? She just didn't want me to get my hopes up too soon, but she was obviously smoking something.

It was denial fueled by ignorance. I wish I could say I decided then and there to prove her wrong, and that my whole mind-set was that of someone determined to heal themselves and walk out of there, but my reaction was simply the result of not knowing any better.

As for God, He was still the furthest thing from my mind. You'd think, sitting there terrified in a cold, sterile room crammed so far deep into the hospital that there wasn't even any sunlight to mark whether it was day or night, that God would have crossed my mind. Nope.

At a time when I needed God most, physically, emotionally, and mentally, I didn't even think to pray. I was in survival mode—it was all about pain and confusion and being drugged. I just wasn't capable of focusing on anything else. I didn't have the luxury of thinking, *I need to pray now*. I can almost picture God standing there in the room, looking at me with "Dude, what are you waiting for?" written all over His face.

As the days went on, the ventilator finally came out, and I could have real conversations with my doctors about what was wrong with me. After five days they moved me out of the ICU, and by then I had the whole story. From the top down, I was a disaster.

My neck was broken clean through at my C6 vertebra. That's the one, almost at the base of the neck, that plays the biggest part in governing how your neck moves. When I fractured it, it shifted outward and bumped out the back of my neck. That break helped me to not feel most of the things that were wrong with me.

The labrum in my right shoulder was torn. The labrum is basically a cuff of cartilage around the shoulder socket that makes the socket "deeper" and helps support the arm bone, while also giving the shoulder a wide range of movement.

In my right elbow I'd ruptured the bursa sac—a small, slippery sack filled with fluid that allows tendons, muscles, and skin to slide easily over bone.

I had two broken ribs on my right side, one of which had pushed into and punctured my right lung. I had a large hematoma in my chest, and contusions on my kidneys, liver, and heart.

My back was broken at my L2 vertebra, the one directly behind the belly button. It's essentially a junction box for the lower extremities—all the nerve pathways run through it—and *broken* is hardly the right word. *Destroyed* is closer to the truth. It had been so badly crushed that it wasn't really even in my back anymore. My L1 and L3 vertebrae had come together—the disc that had been in my spinal column at that point was annihilated, and what was left of my L2 was covering my spinal cord. My spinal canal itself was crushed to just ten percent of its original size. I've since learned that any and all obstructions or pieces of bone in your spinal cord can cause paralysis. I'd not only crushed my spinal cord but, for good measure, I'd covered it with bone debris.

My ankles—both of them—had suffered compound fractures, with bones sticking out of my skin. Medically speaking, I'd broken the talus in each ankle, which is a part of the ankle joint that serves as a primary link between the foot and the leg.

I'd landed mostly on my heels, so my heel bones were shattered and I'd done damage to the metatarsal bones, which are the smaller bones between the middle of the foot and the toes.

Worst of all, I'd hit the ground so hard that my feet had literally exploded. In addition to the bone damage, my feet had split open and most of what should have been inside my feet was now outside, as if my feet had been turned inside out. Dr. Lundy described it as mashed potatoes at the end of a stick. The doctors had kept me knocked out so they could go in and sweep out all the bone and dirt debris from when I'd asked Steve to drag me off the rocks.

I also learned as much as I could about all that the medical team had done to save me.

Dr. Turner and one of his colleagues were actually finishing their shift and leaving when the call came on the radio that the helicopter was bringing me in. They heard the flight nurse's report and turned right around to get ready for what they knew would be a long night.

My first surgery on the night I came in had been to fuse my spine at my L2. They started by filleting me to get to the bone in my back just to see how bad it was. They'd had to harvest bone from my hip and make a block out of it that they then fused with metal rods to the discs above and below that vertebra. They were thinking that they might need to fuse my neck at C6 too, but for the moment, that could wait.

Dr. Lundy had been in charge of my feet. The right one was the worst of the two. It was pretty much a guessing game of what part was supposed to go where—all he really had to work with was a pile of pummeled meat. The right heel bone had disintegrated, to the point that he really felt the foot should have just come off, but I'd already lost so much blood that amputation just wasn't practical. The best he could do was take something called *bone cement*, mix it with the powder that had been my bone and try to re-form something that looked mostly normal. Then everything was screwed together and left to heal. The scar ran from the middle of my arch all the way to my anklebone and toward my Achilles tendon.

As they filled me in on the details, the only thing the doctors left out was their concern that I would never walk again. Even with what they did tell me though, it was more than enough to know that my life was going to change in ways that, less than a week before, I never could have dreamed.

When I was a child, I had a very active imagination. I never really felt like I fit in anywhere. My family used to say I was in my own world most of the time, and for the most part that was true. I used to pretend, when I was lying in my bed at night, that I had some kind of life-threatening illness and everyone would come and visit me. I would lie there pretending to be so sick, and yet so brave. For some strange reason I still can't really explain, there was a kind of fun in it, and in the bed I'd either imagine that I pulled through, or I'd doze off to sleep first.

I thought about that a lot in those first waking days, because this was no longer pretend time. I was really here, and it was the last place I wanted to be. Being brave was the furthest thing from my mind. There was no fun in this, and whenever I dozed off I didn't wake up perfectly healed like in my childhood game. I woke to a horror show of tubes and machines and gray walls and bad lighting.

And the pain, although it was fairly well managed the whole time I was in ICU, was constant. Until your body settles down after that much trauma, your pain sensors are on overload, so while I was in the ICU I had a clicker and every fifteen minutes I could tap it to give myself another morphine hit. Outside of ICU though, they needed to wean me off it, and switched me from an IV to taking pills that I could only get every four hours. The tail end of those four hours became an experience in hell—it was an eternity. Every part of me would hurt in a different way. My feet felt like they were going to explode all over again, and my back felt like someone was jamming a screwdriver into it and wriggling it around. My feet, neck, and back would all throb to the point that it would give me headaches, like a pile driver ramming into my head every second. The bones were just starting to knit together, and all the soft tissue damage was still manifesting, so it felt like my whole body was on fire. It was as if something was chewing on me and never, ever stopping. It got so bad sometimes that I'd just start throwing up. There were times I really thought I wanted to be dead, just so the pain would stop. There was no thought of thanking God that I was alive. It was more like, "Someone please kill me now because it hurts so bad!"

I'd like to think that if I found myself in that same place today, I'd run to God and look to Him to get away from the fear in the pain. But back then, I was just so medicated and busted up, and sometimes so alone, that the pain and the fear were all I could think about. I would lie there in my bed, with friends or family looking on, shaking like a junkie, sweating buckets, waiting for the nurse to come with the drugs. And heaven help them if they were a second late.

In my better moments, I'd do my best to hold up my end of conversations with the slow rotation of friends and family who came to visit, talk, pray for or with me, and try to be encouraging. I learned that Dr. Lundy was a very strong Christian, and that he and his family were praying for me and mine. My co-workers at Group Publishing had put together a huge prayer chain, and thousands of people all around the world were praying for me.

I have to admit, though, sometimes I didn't really want to hear it. It was a very dark time for me; I'll confess, I was a pretty bad Christian. I'd get angry at people who came to visit, and my social skills would go out the window, especially if I was due for a new round of pain meds. Even on my good days, visits had to be short. I only had the strength for about five minutes, and no one ever pushed me.

When the kids came to see me for the first time, though, I wanted to be calm and reassuring for them. I knew Will was too young to really take any of it in, but Mayah was old enough to be frightened by what she saw. When they came into the room, Will just wanted to play with everything, so while Cyndy defended all my tubes and wires, and me, from his grasping fingers, I encouraged Mayah to ask questions. Instead of being afraid, she was curious. She wanted to know what all the machines were, what they did and how they worked. I told her

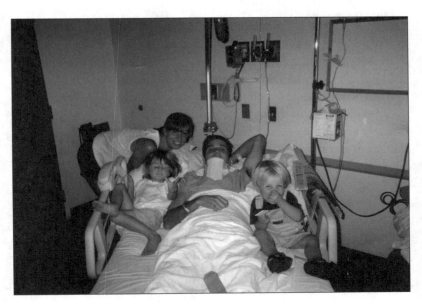

everything about how one machine helped me breathe, and another one told the doctors how fast my heart was beating. Every answer led to more questions, in the way that only a conversation with a four-year-old can, and I was so happy to have that one shred of normalcy.

I wasn't in any kind of routine during those first few days in the hospital. It was way too early for therapy or anything like that. The first time I moved at all was when they tilted me into a sitting position. For the first time I could see what the rest of my body looked like, with the leg braces, the neck brace, and seemingly hundreds of plug-ins. All I could think was *holy crap*.

From there, a big day was when they'd tilt me into a sitting position and wheel me out into the hall. But I was already getting anxious about my recovery. I kept trying to get answers about whether I'd walk again, or when I might actually feel something besides pain below my waist. I couldn't move my toes, and as bad as I was hurting, I had no desire to even try.

I'd gone right to the precipice of death, looked over the edge, and come back to tell the tale. But it was not without a cost, and the full measure of that cost was still being tallied. What it all meant, or would mean, was just a big gray area that was both maddening and frightening. I alternated between a fear of the future so powerful that I couldn't speak, and a barely controlled rage at what had happened to put me in this situation.

> **I alternated between a fear of the future so powerful that I couldn't speak, and a barely controlled rage at what had happened to put me in this situation.**

Everything came down to time windows, and my two crucial windows were eight weeks and eighteen months. Those were the numbers that were going to rule how the rest of my life would unfold. Bones needed eight weeks to heal; and the doctors told me if I didn't get feeling back in the areas where I'd damaged nerves by eighteen months, then I probably never would.

It felt like the time windows were already closing too fast, and no matter where I came out at the end, I was never going to be the man I'd been before. From this point on, my life was going to be a revolving door of pain and scars. My body, the tool I used and relied on and put my trust in more than anything else, especially God, was gone as I'd known it. Forever.

That fact is what scared me the most. The thing I most didn't want to face. And while I was in that place, that's when God spoke to me the loudest.

4

GETTING MY ATTENTION

I had only heard about you before,
but now I have seen you with my own eyes.
I take back everything I said,
and I sit in dust and ashes to show my repentance.

Job 42:5–6

In the hospital my life had become like the movie *Groundhog Day*. Every day the same things happened over and over again. Wake up. Pain meds. Breakfast. Visit from my friend Bill. Therapy. Lunch. Visit with Cyndy and the kids. Hyperbaric treatments. Dinner. More pain meds. Sleep. Wake up and do it all over again.

Mercifully, I don't remember having any dreams in those days. I slept so well that even now I long for the days when I could just sink into that inky black for ten hours every night. You'd think the nights would have been full of nightmares of reliving the accident, but those moments were saved for the waking hours, when a thousand times a day I'd see that yellow anchor shooting away from me just as clearly as if it were happening right then.

Through most of it I was only in one position, on my back, looking up. Usually all I could see was the ceiling, the bars on my bed, and the TV, until someone would come into my field of vision.

The highlights were visits from my friend Bill Fisher and the time with my family. Bill would come every day around 8:30 and we'd talk about all kinds of normal things. Never about the accident or my recovery for more than a few minutes. When he'd visit I could feel like a regular person again. His visits would jump-start the creative side of my brain again and I was always thankful for that.

The time with the kids was always a joy, but it came at a cost. I didn't ever want the kids to worry about me or think they couldn't play around me, so I welcomed it when they crawled all over me in the bed. Sometimes it would've been hard to imagine a worse form of torture, but I tried to wear a smile through it all and not say anything. Things had to be as normal as possible, no matter how fragile I'd become.

And I was fragile—physically and mentally. In the fabric that was everything my life had become there was always some thread of gratitude for being alive, for still being with my family, but as the days wore on with little prospect of change, that thread got more and more obscured. I was alive, but my feet didn't work, my neck and arm were completely wrecked, and my back was broken so badly no one could even guess what my life was going to be like. It seemed like every day the doctors would find something else that was wrong with me. As much as I didn't want the accident to define me, there were many stark moments when I'd take a mental step back from everything and see my life for what it was. It was like a book where every page has the exact same words, bound by a chronic pain that connected each day to the next.

My whole identity, as a photographer, a husband, a dad, a climber—especially a climber—was gone. What was I now to my wife? To my kids? I had no idea who I was anymore, or who I was going to be. My whole life I'd been someone who could train my body to do anything I wanted it to do; now it took three people and a winch just to get me to the bathroom.

A journal entry I wrote around that time said it all:

> Things are changing fast, and my doctors are not sure what can be saved and not saved, and that scares me more than I can say. I used to ask God what His plan for me was. I'm not at all sure why He saved me. I can only see the very near future. I have no long-term thoughts. I used to wonder about the future and if I was up to the challenges in front of me. I never thought of this. Now I fight fear, pain, and loneliness with an uncertain future. I hear and see the strain this

all has on my wife and kids, and I want to die. I feel totally helpless, like my whole world is slipping past me and I can't do anything to stop it.

I'm not sure who I am now. Climbing was a big part of who I am for thirteen years and I was good at it. Better than most, and that had a feeling of power behind it that I liked. The feeling of being good at an athletic thing. It felt good to be able to do things others can't. Now I think of being high up on a rock wall and all I see is the rope and that anchor and how it looked as I was falling away from it. Why didn't I double-check Steve? Why didn't he?

I worry if I'm not a climber anymore—climbing's been such a huge part of who we are as a couple—will Cyndy still feel the same way about me?

I began to withdraw. I was surrounded by friends, co-workers, people in the climbing community, and even strangers who'd send letters and cards. Everyone told me how much they cared about me and how they were there for me, but I couldn't explain what was happening in my mind to any of them, not even my wife. I felt like I was in this pit, trying to call for someone to lift me out, but no one could understand me. I needed help to do everything, and trying to communicate what that was like to anyone was impossible, so it became easier not to communicate at all. There were times I really enjoyed being left alone.

I wouldn't say I was falling into depression; it was more like confusion. My whole existence was being built around my next dose of pain meds. I would lie there and wonder, *What am I supposed to do with all of this? What am I supposed to do now?* I thought about that constantly, and more than once I brought it up with God. I made sure He understood that if this was all there was going to be, then that really wasn't going to work for me.

I grew up in the Catholic Church and, like many fellow attendees, grew up with religion but not a deep and abiding faith. The whole idea of a personal relationship with God was not talked about much, so by the time I was out of college and working as a photographer, spiritual things didn't even rate as being ignored; they were forgotten. In 1994 I made a trip to Colorado to visit with friends and fell so in love with the state that when I got home, I bought a copy of the *Denver Post* and started looking for jobs. It wasn't long before I saw an ad from Group Publishing looking for a photographer, and I applied. I remember they knew I wasn't a Christian at that point; the owner even went so far as to say, "You know, this is a Christian company, right?" In all truth, my game plan was to get them to hire me so I could move to Colorado, climb as much as I wanted, look for another job and then quit Group when I found something. My opinion of Christians was pretty low. None of them were people I wanted to hang out with. They always came off as being a little too fake for me. The whole "God is in control" thing sounded more like a general cop-out than anything else.

My first few weeks at Group went about as you might expect when a worldly non-Christian gets air-dropped into a Christian environment. Picture Snoop Dogg going to work for Focus on the Family.

Despite a rough start (in the first week my boss had to sit me down and have a talk about my constant swearing), I came to like the job and my co-workers. Two of them were also climbers and, to their credit, they invested some time in me. They took me aside and explained the ground rules of the workplace, and they invited me climbing. The more time we spent together, the more I came to appreciate how they lived their lives. There was nothing fake about them. They had this genuine peace about them; and the more I saw of it, the more I began to want that for myself. Then one day I was doing a photo shoot at a church in Fort Collins and the pastor did an altar call. At first I stood there thinking about how bizarre it all seemed, but as I listened, everything suddenly started to click. Everything my co-workers had been talking about and exemplifying in their own lives suddenly made so much sense, and I responded. Cyndy and I were just starting to date at the time, and I remember being worried that she'd think I'd turned into some kind of wing nut, but my fears could not have been more misplaced. We became new believers together. It was a wonderful way to begin our marriage.

That's all a long way of saying that as I lay in the hospital recovering, I knew all about the idea of God having a plan for us. I knew God was real; I knew Christ had died on the cross for us and was resurrected; I knew all about how God had started a good work in me. But in those many times when I was alone and confused, that knowledge provided no reassurance. I tried to interrogate God. *What had happened, and why? What was I supposed to do with all of this? How was this part of some great, good plan?* I saw no good in it; all I saw was a big ball of crushed bone and meat that used to be my body.

While I did think that being dead would be better sometimes, I never actually wished I were dead. I was glad to be alive and with my family, but I couldn't help thinking that things would have been easier if I had died. I certainly wouldn't have to deal with the laundry list of things wrong with me. I asked God about it over and over again, but there were no answers. I'd lie there, in a world where there was no tomorrow or yesterday, just this present moment in the midst of a routine that would be repeated again and again, and I'd wonder, *Is this it? Is this my life from now on? Am I going to spend the rest of my life in a bed or a chair?* I'd gotten tired of asking my doctors. They either didn't know or would give me just enough information to think they were keeping me happy. So I kept asking God, but He wasn't showing me the way. To me at that time, He was being completely silent.

I never stopped asking the questions, but I could only stare at the ceiling, waiting for an answer, for so long. Sometimes, if I stayed really still and didn't move at all, the pain would be more tolerable and I'd feel almost normal, but it never lasted long and I needed something else to occupy my thoughts. Other than the TV, my only real source of entertainment or distraction came in the form of whatever was within easy reach on the small table by my bed. Sometimes it'd be a book or a magazine, sometimes cards and letters from friends or family. Cyndy and the hospital staff managed to keep a good rotation of stuff on that table, until one day I looked over and saw a small daily devotional.

I'd seen it before—it was part of a bigger care package an old friend had sent me out of the blue—and I'd rolled my eyes at it. Despite becoming a believer, I still had pretty strong opinions about "some Christians" and I'd attached the concept of devotionals to *those* people, those "cardboard Christians" so full of joy and hypocrisy. To me, daily devotionals had everything in common with that image of Christianity and I wanted nothing to do with it. I didn't need to devote myself to anything; I just needed to get through the day.

On that particular day in August, I was bored out of my mind. It was one of those days where time was just crawling by and I got tired of watching the fluorescent lights flicker above me. Desperate for anything, I reached over and grabbed the devotional, *Grace for the Moment* by Max Lucado. I rolled my eyes again, then cracked it open.

It was August, but as I opened the book, the first page I went to was July 21, the day of the accident. As I read the first sentence, my heart nearly stopped.

"How far do you want God to go in getting your attention?" it said. And the second sentence hit me even harder. "If God has to choose between your eternal safety and your earthly comfort, which do you hope he chooses?"

In that instant, I was being called out to face the truth of my relationship with the creator of the universe and, with the same mind-searing clarity I had on the day of the fall, I saw how entirely superficial that relationship had been.

I'd been saved, yes, and by every textbook definition I was a Christian, but God had never really had my attention. God was little more than an accessory in a busy life filled with other priorities, carefully put into the spots where I wanted Him and kept out of the places I didn't. My walk with God had been on cruise control almost from day one, and I had nothing more than a faith of convenience, accented by childish prayers to help me do well and be healthy. I realized I'd treated my relationship with God like a vending machine where I'd put in a few token prayers and expect some kind of prize to come out.

> **My walk with God had been on cruise control almost from day one, and I had nothing more than a faith of convenience, accented by childish prayers to help me do well and be healthy.**

I thought about how I had worked hard to fit God into my life where it was most convenient for me, and wherever there was a conflict it was as if God was just the kid I played with because he had cool toys. I saw how I had always put my faith and trust into my own body, and the fall had taken away the one thing I had put the most stock in, myself. It wasn't that God had plucked me off of that cliff; I'd been overly confident and gotten lax and for that I had lost everything I thought was important.

The more I thought about it, the more I saw my relationship with God in stark reality. I saw myself as a very sinful, egocentric person who had never really tried to live his life as a reflection of the love God has shown all of us, and I felt embarrassed, ashamed, and even horrified.

Mostly, I felt like a complete idiot.

As I read on, the devotional spoke about God's relentless pursuit of us, and how He does whatever it takes to get our attention because He doesn't want any of us to be lost. The book felt very heavy in my hand, and the room around me felt very small. God finally showed me what my life was before the fall, and was giving me the choice to make it something different after the fall.

I put the book down, and for the first time since the day I came to Christ, I really, really prayed.

The first thing I did was apologize. I apologized for relegating Him to third or fourth place in my life, for being the very kind of "fake" Christian I had so looked down upon, and for being such a jerk. I put it all on the table and asked for His forgiveness. I stopped trying to understand what had happened and put my life in His hands. I stopped asking God what *I* was supposed to do with this broken body, and instead put my trust in *Him* to make me into what He wanted me to be. I accepted that I was so broken at this point that the only way I'd get rebuilt was if He was the one rebuilding me. All I asked was that He point me in the right direction.

There were no voices when I prayed, only silence. But I felt Him. I felt God's Spirit in me, and it stirred me so deeply that even now, as I think of that moment, it has a physical effect on me. It's electrifying, and even just the memory of it helps shift the entire world into focus.

> **With everything out in the open at last, I had an incredible feeling of peace.**

As I finished praying, I again asked God to show me the things He wanted me to do and that He take my accident and use it to glorify His kingdom. With everything out in the open at last, I had an incredible feeling of peace. It was like I'd been telling a lie for years, but the truth had finally come out and I didn't need to try to hide it any more. It was all in the past now and time for a fresh start. I truly felt God's grace, and it was much more than grace for the moment. I felt like my wheels had been spinning right up until the moment I'd opened the devotional and now suddenly I was getting some traction and gaining some momentum. I had moved from simply knowing *about* God to really *knowing* God.

Not surprisingly, the boredom of that day vanished. I spent most of it in reflection, alternating between beating myself up for being so arrogant and stupid, and reveling in God's grace. When Cyndy came in later I showed her the book and we talked for a long time about it, about what I'd experienced, and how we both really wanted the same thing: for God to lead both of us as we made decisions.

The feeling and the excitement stayed with me until the evening pain meds kicked in and I fell asleep. I don't remember dreaming; as with so many other nights, it was like my body simply switched off and when I awoke the next morning I was in a ton of pain again, just like always.

Same pain, different day. I remember thinking, *Huh, I thought God was going to step into my life and make things real clear, instead I'm just stepping into the routine again.* Pain can be very distracting . . . it's hard to listen when you're in pain, but I didn't question God. I just let it be, and that afternoon, the very day after I had asked God to use my accident to glorify His kingdom, God took me up on it.

My friend and boss, Thom Schultz came to visit me. He said he had an idea, but wasn't sure why he'd had it. He wanted to film my recovery and use it in some way to help people. How he'd do that was a big question mark, but he just knew there would be a need for it and wanted to ask my permission. I figured at the very least it would be a good way for Mayah and Will to someday understand what had happened to their daddy both physically and spiritually, so I agreed. We made a plan for getting started the next day. I'd have a two-person film crew following me around for the rest of my recovery. It would be like having my own reality show.

That was only the beginning of God really working in my life, however. The next day the phone rang. It was a writer from Focus on the Family (FOTF). He wanted to know if he could visit later that week and get my story for an article he was writing in one of their men's magazines. Bear in mind that in terms of how the media looks at the concept of time, my accident was old news by then. Until that day though, no one had come to me with an interest of hearing and sharing my story. And what was funny was that when I had prayed the day before, I had asked God to make the path clear, but I had also asked Him to please not make me talk about my faith; I wasn't comfortable doing that. Here in the midst of this great big epiphany I was still trying to dictate the terms of my faith; I can almost picture God laughing out loud and shaking His head at that one. I'd asked God to use me for His purpose, and He was going hold me to it.

Here in the midst of this great big epiphany I was still trying to dictate the terms of my faith; I can almost picture God laughing out loud and shaking His head at that one.

After Thom and the writers from FOTF, TV crews and newspaper reporters started showing up. It became a slow parade of interested onlookers, and every single one of them wanted to talk to me about my faith. It was impossible not to see the hand of God at work, and as it went on, I came to really appreciate the chance to sort of reflect on my relationship with God through the course of the various interviews.

I came to realize that I didn't want to hide behind my mistakes. It was true confession time. I wanted people to know I'd had a very superficial faith. I wanted to talk about the things I'd done wrong and what I was going to do about it. And as I spoke to people, eventually they would all ask me the same question, "Why do you think you survived?"

To be clear, I still really had no idea what God had in mind for me. It wasn't like I'd had this sudden vision and my whole life's path was laid out before me. I'd only taken a few small steps in a long progression. I couldn't answer that question with grandiose designs about launching a ministry and reaching others with the message of God's love for us. I could only tell them that God had plans for my life and what those plans were I didn't know, but one thing was certain: He didn't want me to die that day.

Saying that, and feeling the truth of it, made me want to get healed to whatever extent God wanted me to be. I wanted to get started on whatever God's work was for me and get on with whatever my life was meant to be from that point on.

I also knew that before I could really do that, I had to make peace with Steve. It wasn't that I was angry with him—it was more like I had to make a conscious decision that I was never going to get angry at him, that I was never going to let myself go there. Without that, I would just be stuck in place. I knew if I didn't let go of any temptation to be mad at God or at Steve, all I would do is burn in anger and then just plain burn out. I needed to choose between being angry about my situation or getting better.

Steve came to visit me every day in the hospital, and in a slow, delicate dance, we talked through what happened. I could see Sundance Buttress in his eyes every time we spoke. It was one of the few times I could get beyond what was happening with me and empathize with what someone else was going through. Steve hadn't been hurt that day, but he'd gone through an unimaginable horror. He had endured his own very real trauma. And he blamed himself for it.

It might be easy for anyone on the outside to think he was at fault. Unfortunately, a lot of people who didn't know any better decided that since he was the one who was supposed to be holding the rope, he was to blame. He took a lot of unfair heat from it. More than once, he would sit in my hospital room and cry, saying he felt responsible, and I would cry right along with him because I just couldn't convince him that he wasn't.

That wasn't me just being charitable and forgiving. It's fact. If I had done what I was supposed to do, and said what I was supposed to say, the accident would not have happened. That's not just my opinion either. In the conclusion of his official investigation report, U.S. Park Ranger William Alexander said it all in one sentence: "Based on current evidence and interviews, I suspect that DeMartino's fall was the result of poor communications between the two climbers."

Even more important, Steve Gorham saved my life that day. I am still here, my wife still has a husband, and my kids still have a father today because of him. He truly was one of the miracles on that mountain.

He kept his cool and stayed focused. Most people would have stood paralyzed with shock at what he witnessed, but he went right into action. It was as if he instantly had a plan and knew what to do. He put the tourniquet on me. He found his phone in his backpack. He told the rescuers where to find us. He stayed with me and did everything he could to make me comfortable.

I explained all that to him as we talked over the weeks. I needed him to know that wherever this road was going, he and I were okay.

He listened, but I could tell it was a hard sell for him. I think it was very hard for him to get out of a place where he wanted to fix everything, but was powerless to do it. I'd been in that same place for a long time, only I eventually turned it all over to God. After that I wasn't burdened with trying to make things right anymore. There was only moving forward. I prayed for Steve to see God in all of this, and that only by letting go of his guilt, and giving it to God, would he feel free again.

By the time I left the hospital, I think Steve was willing to accept that the accident was just that, an accident brought about by a series of small events that added up to something terrible. But I don't know if he really made peace with what happened. While we stayed close after I left the hospital, we never talked about the accident again. He went back to his life and worked hard to try to put it behind him. I moved home and worked on getting better.

Of course, God works according to His own timetable, as anyone who has ever prayed about anything can appreciate. He had more trials for me to go through. "More deserts to cross," as the saying goes. I would still deal with pain every day of my life, from the moment I opened my eyes in the morning, and I would never be physically whole again. It would be more than eighteen months before I'd really even be able to walk again on my own, and when I did, I'd have to do it without one of my legs.

5

THE HEALING ORDEAL

The trials I had yet to endure were mental, physical, and emotional. I wish I could say I was bright and cheery with every new day following my great personal epiphany, but I'd be lying. There really is a difference between joy and happiness, at least from a Christian perspective, and in fact joy has little to do with happiness. My new, true joy came from a deep and abiding confidence in the presence of God. That gave me a new attitude of peace, but I was still the same flawed man who had fallen off that cliff. There was no denying it.

Instead of happiness, it seemed like every new day brought more bad news. It began to set in that my body had a long, long way to go before it was ever going to be done healing. And "done healing" would not mean "healed." There would come a point where my body would not get any better, and whatever shape I was in at that point was going to be the best it was going to get.

Above all else, there was the pain.

It was like a tide; it would come in and go out. But the evenings were the worst. All day long I'd be somewhere around a four on the pain scale, but by 6:00 or so the pain would twist its way up to a seven or eight. I'd be lying in my bed with my feet hurting so bad that I was shaking, and I was basically helpless until the med cart finally came around. I'd try to do the pain management technique they'd taught me about visualizing the pain. In my mind I'd see it as this hot, searing white light, and I'd mentally try to fold it up into smaller pieces until I could put it in a box. In the box it would be enclosed and I could try to talk myself into believing that with the pain enclosed, I couldn't feel it.

I'm sure that works for some people and I do see merit in it, but while I was in the hospital it never worked. The pain was so visceral that visualizing it only made me more aware of it. And while pain takes such an enormous toll on you, that's not only a physical toll. Fighting it every day, knowing that it's coming and might never go away, would open up some of the darkest places in my mind, where there would be nothing but despair at what had happened to me . . . what had *become* of me. It was a part of my mind that showed me only a future with no hope. It was more than just depressing; its power to suck me in could be terrifying.

Every day, often several times a day, I had to force my mind to focus on something else, to run away from that dark place. It wasn't a matter of just trying to have positive thoughts; ultimately it was a survival decision. It would have been only too easy to get lost in that dark place and become a completely different person forever. But I knew that's not who I wanted to be, and so as I dealt with the constant physical pain, my mind and spirit were in overdrive, trying to stay focused on the right things and to resist the temptation to give myself up for lost. The effort was exhausting.

> **As I dealt with the constant physical pain, my mind and spirit were in overdrive, trying to stay focused on the right things and to resist the temptation to give myself up for lost. The effort was exhausting.**

When night came, and along with it the pain meds that I knew would take exactly twenty minutes to kick in, I'd be so worn out from the daily fight that I'd just pass out. The sleep was a reprieve, but with each waking morning the pain would come back in a rush, as if it wanted to make up for lost time, and the whole fight would begin again.

As for my healing process, it seemed to be going backward instead of forward. My cuts and bruises were better, but the deep damage was still there, especially my right foot. And the doctor I had working on me was hardly a source of comfort. I nicknamed him "Dr. Macabre" because he never had anything encouraging to say. In the very first hour he met me, he told me my foot was going to have to come off.

The very thought was abhorrent to me. I could fathom the idea that I'd have to find and adjust to a new normal with my body, but no way was that going to mean cutting off pieces of it. As long as I had all my limbs, there was reason to believe I'd be able to do all the things

I loved—skiing, hiking, biking, and yes, even climbing. Without my foot I wouldn't be able to do any of it. Losing my foot would be a life sentence to a prison where everything that made living enjoyable was within reach but impossible to grasp.

On the night I'd come in, the doctors had done everything, including rebuilding my foot from nothing, to try to save it. They must have thought it was worth saving, and I held on to that, even as I faced a daily terror when the doctors came in.

The only way they could keep tabs on it was to check under the hood every morning. Imagine an L-shaped line going down the outside of your ankle and then across along the outside of your foot, near the bottom. That's the kind of incision I had on my right foot. Every day I lived with the fear that they'd come in to clean my foot and after one look they'd tell me it was infected. It was like that part of *The Princess Bride* where the Dread Pirate Roberts told Wesley every night, "Good work. Sleep well. I'll most likely kill you in the morning." Of course, in the movie, that line was hilarious. My situation was nowhere near funny.

For the longest time, they wouldn't even let me see it. It was just this thing on the end of my body that was silently dictating what the rest of my life was going to be like. I got good at reading their faces, and in those first days it was clear that things weren't going well. It was extremely frustrating. Why couldn't they just get that thing to heal? They'd tell me all about how that part of the body doesn't get the best blood flow; "It's just a part of your body that doesn't do well," I think Dr. Macabre said one day. Oh, he was perfect.

They decided to start me on Hyperbaric Oxygen treatment, or HBO, to try to accelerate the healing process and improve the chances of saving my foot. Only they just kept calling it "HBO," and I was seriously sitting there wondering how watching movies was going to help.

What I learned was that HBO is like an air pressure chamber. They slide you into this clear plastic tube and double the amount of oxygen in the air around you. The theory is that the increase in oxygen can double the speed and progress of the healing process.

"There's a good chance this will make you heal better," the doctors told me as I nodded intelligently and tried not to let my excitement look too much like desperation. I tried to show an attitude of "sure man, whatever," as if I wasn't too concerned. I'd have chugged down chicken blood if someone said it would help.

I was a little apprehensive when they first wheeled me into the HBO room. It's all the way at the bottom of the hospital, so they'd wheel me to the elevator and then along a basement hallway. The room itself was nothing special. It was really just a slightly glamorized triple-occupancy hospital room with three large clear tubes where the beds should be and the requisite TV screens mounted above each.

There was no dry run when I got to the room for my first appointment either—no test run or even a transition period. They just rolled me right into this clear plastic coffin and shut the door. I'm not a big fan of small spaces. I wouldn't go as far as to say I'm claustrophobic, but small spaces do scare me. If it had been anything other than a clear tube, things might not have gone so well.

Right away, I could feel the pressure increasing in my ears, so I started equalizing with my nose. They had a blanket in there, for which I'm thankful, because I'll never forget how cold it was in that tube.

They told me at the time that my HBO regimen would begin that day and continue for thirteen weeks. Each HBO treatment would last for two hours and I'd have to stay in the tube for the entire cycle. After the first day, it was never interesting again.

As a photographer, I'm a visual person. Visual cues get my brain working its creative muscles as I try to frame up shots or compose settings. I can't stand color monotony, which of course, is something hospitals thrive on. I love color and texture, and to suddenly be injected into all that sterility . . . I was being deprived. I couldn't even wear my own clothes; I had to wear a hospital gown, which was white. All the doctors wore white. The rooms were white. The nurses' shoes were white. My world was like a kid's snow cone with all the flavor juice sucked away through the straw.

I won't say it drove me crazy, but the monotony of color was a perfect match to the monotony of my daily routine.

The trips to the HBO room were the exception. As they wheeled me down on the gurney, I could only look up. The ceiling was white, of course, as were the fluorescent lights that flashed by like the stripes on a road. Then it was down an elevator, which had some strangely appealing shades of gray, followed by a left turn down the hallway that led to the white HBO room.

They were doing some construction work in that hallway, so all the ceiling tiles were gone. I could see into the ceiling itself, and into the structure of the flooring above. I could see all the pipes, girders, and conduit wires that were usually hidden. It was the one thing in my day that was actually interesting to look at, a refreshing stripe of color and detail unlike anything else in my field of vision.

Once the HBO treatment started, they'd pipe in movies to help pass the time (so watching movies really did have something to do with it after all), but even with that I used to equate HBO with jail time. And I had to do it five days a week. It was like being in isolation, and I hated it.

Except for the day I met the young man, probably in his early twenties, who I thought of as "the kid."

The first thing I noticed about him was how pissed off he was. He had an Ilizarov fixator on his leg. That's the big metal halo apparatus that gets pinned into the bone on either side of a bad break, and all the rings are connected to each other outside the body by threaded rods attached by adjustable nuts. It looks like some kind of torture device, and—considering that as the bone heals the nuts have to be turned four times a day to increase the distance between the rings— I've heard it lives up to its image.

I had only to look at the kid's face to know that, but he only had to look at me to realize that he wasn't so bad off. He'd eventually heal and walk out of there. At the time, I couldn't even sit up.

That was the first time my own injuries actually helped someone feel better about theirs. I wasn't keenly aware of that going on at the time, but it explains a lot about why he and I started talking.

While living in the hospital, I had this belief that everyone who worked there was trying to help me. So as long as the pain was under control, I found it easy to have a positive attitude with most people, especially the staff. He seemed just the opposite.

We shared the same room every morning for a few days, and I think boredom and morbid curiosity eventually overtook him. He gave me a good looking over, like someone driving by the scene of a traffic accident, until our eyes met. I thought he might look away, but he held my gaze and, with a slight nod of acknowledgment for a fellow prisoner, said, "So what happened to you?" I gave him the Reader's Digest version and was a little surprised at how easy it was to tell the story, as if I wanted him to understand that whatever he'd endured really paled in comparison.

That kicked off a conversation that was serialized over the next several days. I found out he had just moved out to Colorado from Nebraska. He'd moved to Fort Collins to go to school. One day after school he'd been riding his motorcycle home or to work and had been hit by a car. His leg was a train wreck to be sure, but what really made him angry wasn't the injury. It was that he was all alone.

Everyone he knew was back in Nebraska, and not one friend or family member had come out to visit, check on him, or even just be around to help out with things. He was dealing with everything by himself. We never talked about his attitude, but there's no doubt that his ability to see that I was a much bigger train wreck than he was made him feel better. And I encouraged him to think that way.

I remember after our first conversation the nurse had come over to me and told me how surprised she was. Apparently, the kid never talked to anyone. As I look back, I see the seeds of my current ministry to victims of trauma in those early conversations. At the time I wasn't thinking along those lines at all; I think I've just always been good at helping people keep perspective on things. The fact that it comes so naturally to me just convinces me all the more that God was at work throughout all of this.

I'm not sure what happened with the kid beyond that because, after he had been in the hospital only two weeks, they told me it was time to leave. Neither the hospital nor my insurance company could let me stay there any longer. I'd reached a point where I didn't require that level of care anymore. I was stable enough to move, I was rested and sutured, and it was time for them to focus on people who weren't.

Unfortunately, they only gave me one day's notice. They simply came into my room one day and told me they were going to have to move me. To say the news was disheartening is like saying Israel and Palestine have their differences. I was in shock.

How could they be done with me when I myself was nowhere near "done"? I couldn't walk, I couldn't feel anything below my right knee, the pain was still managing *me* if we were all being honest about it, and I'd been given no assurance that I was going to keep my foot.

And I had to leave? It felt as if the doctors had just given up on me as a lost cause.

They weren't kicking me out on the street, of course, and they didn't need to notice the frantic look in my eyes to know I wasn't ready to go home. I was stable, but I was still very fragile. The only option was a rehab center where I could get extended care. Cyndy had been working with the hospital staff for the past few days to find the best one and had settled on Center Rehab, only a few miles from the hospital.

I'll never forget the next morning when they came for me. Procedure probably dictated that they tell me again what was happening, that I was being moved to an extended care facility. "You're going to get the best care you need for however long it takes!" They were trying to be encouraging, I know, but the only thing that registered with me was the "however long it takes" part. While my perception of my recovery had always been one that involved some kind of timetable, albeit one with no guaranteed outcomes, there was still an end date out there. With those words, that was gone.

Shock and fear and confusion set in all over again, to the point I shut down and wasn't aware of what was happening around me. Then they sat me in the wheelchair.

It had always sent bolts of white-hot pain through me whenever they sat me up, but there had always been the prospect of lying back down again. In the wheelchair there was no escape. I had to stay sitting up and the pain got so bad I felt like passing out.

And then for the first time since the accident, I was outside.

The photographer in me was not on duty or I would have taken the time to notice the colors, which were like an onslaught compared to the industrial white of the hospital. The pain was blinding, and what should have been refreshing, even pleasant, was simply washed out by that pain, and by the fact that I was experiencing the lowest and most depressing time of my recovery and of my life.

I'd been cautiously optimistic all this time, but I'd been in the safe confines of my hospital room and the HBO chamber. Even when they occasionally rolled my bed and my entourage of tubes and machines into the hallway I was still well insulated from the rigors of actual travel or movement. I hadn't thought that simply being wheeled out into the parking lot would be so difficult and, as a result, so emotionally crushing.

And it got worse. The van was waiting outside. A young guy in his twenties jumped out and came over to the side. It was one of those lift vans, and as he lowered it so the orderly could wheel me in, he couldn't resist. He took a look at me.

I was in a full, high-back wheelchair with huge, plastic walking casts on both legs. I had a full back brace and neck brace. By all appearances, I was only being held together by an outer layer of plaster, metal, and plastic. I saw him looking at me, and what I saw in his eyes made me want to cry out in despair: *pity.*

Until that day I'd wondered what my life was going to be like. The ride in the wheelchair answered that question. The look in that man's eyes told me everything. This *was* my life.

I wept all the way to the rehab center.

It was a ten-minute ride and I was in every imaginable kind of pain for every second of it. Cyndy was with me and doing her best to be a source of comfort. This amazing woman, who'd been giving everything of herself for a month already, dug deeper to try to give more.

"This is just the next step," she told me. "This is okay. We're going to keep going forward through this." It was like she was throwing a rope and calling to me at the bottom of a deep, dark hole but I couldn't see it or hear her over the sound of my own screaming.

I calmed down as they wheeled me into Center Rehab, but my mood didn't get any better. There were to be no good emotions that day, just fear and depression, which would govern most of my life for the next three months.

The new routine set in quickly. I was in a different place, but once again, every day was the same. First thing every morning after I woke up was breakfast. They tried to persuade me to eat in the dining commons with everyone else, but I couldn't do it. The truth is I couldn't stand looking at those other people. It was the kind of place where everyone wore slippers. All the time. I was convinced that few of them would ever be going home again. The mere sight of them stoked my fears about my own future, and redoubled my insistence that I didn't belong in this kind of life.

After breakfast I'd get visitors; mostly friends, co-workers, and well-wishers from the climbing world. Occasionally the youth pastor from our church paid a visit, but beyond him there was not a lot from our church congregation. That's not their fault though.

At the time we were going to a megachurch; I think about three thousand people attended there. And if God had been just an accessory in my life, well, church was only for when I felt like putting the accessory on. We'd attend fairly regularly but, as anyone knows, there's a big difference between attending a church and being involved in it. We weren't in a small group, we weren't supporting any specific church ministry, and we weren't even members. I once heard of a pastor in a large church saying to his people that if they weren't involved in the church in some way, such as a small group, their church community would fail them when they needed it most. What he meant was that by being isolated and unplugged, they weren't giving the church the opportunity to do anything but to fail them.

So while my employer launched a prayer chain and had thousands of people around the world praying for me within twenty-four hours of the accident, the fact that I never even got a visit from the senior pastor of my own church was no one's fault but mine.

In the rehab center, I'd also get a daily visit from doctors who wanted to see if I was getting any feeling back in my right leg. I never looked forward to these visits. I couldn't even move my toes, much less feel anything, so I knew things were bad. You should know what your toes are doing.

Their test involved rolling this little spiky wheel, like a pizza cutter with points all around the edge, over my skin. I wasn't allowed to see where they were testing; I'd just have to tell them where I could feel it. They'd start on my hands first and I'd tell them which finger they were testing. Then they'd take the bandages off my feet and roll it along my legs. The very first time, I was completely honest about it. And I could see on their faces that they weren't happy with what I was saying. So the next time I started lying.

I'd tell them I could feel something but they caught on to me quickly. They'd ask where I could feel it and I could only guess at where the wheel really was. At my best I wouldn't actually feel anything as much as sense it . . . the feeling was like wearing a big heavy coat and having someone lightly run their finger along the back. When I would guess wrong they would try pushing the wheel a little harder, or they'd move it to an area where I really could feel it and then roll it back to the dead zone. That's really what it was. I'd feel the wheel rolling along and then nothing. Nothing at all.

They were always very supportive and encouraging; they'd tell me I was doing great and all that, but I knew I was failing. I wasn't fooling anyone by lying about feeling the wheel, but in my own way I guess I thought I could fake them out. I thought that if I could guess right that would mean I was getting better, and if I could convince them (and myself) that I was getting better, then maybe I really would. It was a mind over matter kind of thing. That, and I just needed some good news, even if I had to manufacture it on my own. I was given fresh servings of bad news every day; every day it was like they took something else away from me. Every day brought one less reason to have hope.

Most of all, I was so desperate to keep my foot. I just needed something to go my way, and so I grew to hate that vicious, soul-eating, little wheel.

My foot flap still wasn't showing great signs of healing after the move, so every day after breakfast and maybe visits from friends or family, they'd wheel me out into the van for a trip back to the hospital and into the HBO coffin. Dr. Macabre was always there to rain on my parade, which, despite how impossible it first seemed, actually made the HBO visits worse.

I'd get back to the rehab center in time for lunch—alone in my room. The food was no source of comfort—ever. After lunch it was off to occupational therapy, which I hated more than anything else. They had me write, count, read, and do a whole bunch of rudimentary things that frankly weren't much of a problem. The most irritating thing of all was this little plastic "toy" called an "incentive spirometer" or simply an "inspirometer." It had a small tube connected by a hose to a chamber that had a small plastic ball in it. I had to put the tube in my mouth and inhale as much as I could, as forcefully as I could. The stronger and better I was at this, the higher up the little ball would go and remain. The goal was to get it to float up to a certain level and stay there for most of the breath.

I found it moronic, and I did a very poor job of hiding it. My goal was to get back to walking on my own, so I saw no value or purpose in sucking air and floating a stupid little ball. I didn't care about lung capacity, I cared about making my legs work, and I said as much to my occupational therapist. She was quick to pick up on my frustration, and after only three or four sessions said we could quit and pick it up again when it was time for me to go home. I liked the sound of that, on more than one level.

Next came Shelly, my physical therapist. She is a very loving person, but everything that woman did to me hurt. She'd start innocently enough. She'd sit with me and tell me what we were going to be working on that day, and I'd listen to it all with what could only be described as morbid curiosity. Then two orderlies would lift me in a crane—casts, braces, and all—to a wheelchair, and off we'd go to the torture chamber.

For the first sessions she'd simply wheel me to the therapy room, which I remember being a very nice color of white, and from the chair she'd transfer me to a mattress on the floor. At first that simple transfer was all I could handle; I'd be so wiped out that they'd just lift me right back into the bed and that'd be it for my part.

As we progressed she added thirty-minute beatings to the routine, with deep tissue rubs on my back, legs, hands, elbows, whatever part of me she needed to drill into on a given day. Her job was to break down scar tissue and she was good at it. Sometimes as she worked certain sections, I could hear the scar tissue cracking and popping inside me like some 1940s thug cracking his knuckles. By kneading up and down, then across the scarred and injured areas, she progressed all over, hurting me the whole time.

After administering a good beating, she'd move on to the therabands to help get my joints used to moving again. She'd wrap one around a leg or an arm and my job was to pull against it, working on strength, stretching, and mobility. Pulling all that tight skin and scarring was incredibly painful, and I'd have to do a certain number of repetitions to make her happy.

I knew what she was doing had a purpose, but all I could think about was how much it hurt and how I could think of a million places I'd rather be than in this room with this woman. More than once, after she'd bent and twisted me around, I'd just sit and cry because it hurt so bad.

Still, those sessions were ideal for a task-oriented person like me. If I wanted to walk out of this facility and into a normal life, I had to do this. I'd hate every minute of it, but I'd love what it was doing for my body.

Every couple of days she'd change it up, so I never really knew what was coming. I think that lack of knowing was good in some ways, but for the most part it etched a wince on my face.

If there was one pleasant constant to our sessions, it was going outside afterwards. It was summertime, so it was always nice and toasty, and it felt so good. Just the contact of fresh air on my skin after all that time in the sterile, stagnant, iodine-laced air of the hospital was enough to make me want to get out of my wheelchair and run. Shelly would give me an overall assessment of what she'd done that day and what it meant for my body and its healing. I was still plagued with feelings of failure, but she was always so positive. Over and over she would tell me that it was all about making a steady stream of small improvements rather than trying to make a great leap all at once.

I couldn't help reminding myself that that was exactly how I had experienced my rescue—in small servings—and how grateful I'd been not to know the whole picture. It's also a lot like climbing a big wall. You do it pitch by pitch, not all in one jump. You have to pace your-

self, physically and mentally. In that sense, my climbing had prepared me for this.

The conclusion of each session with Shelly was joy in itself, but it was a joy made whole when Cyndy and the kids would come visit. We'd all stay outside enjoying the afternoon air, talking, playing, and feeling almost like a normal family. Those visits were often the highlight of my day.

Seeing Cyndy especially was a huge lift. After so much time together, and doing so much together, now to only see her for a little while each day was hard on me. She's my best friend, and I was really missing her. We'd basically been apart in all but the most superficial way for a month and a half.

While Cyndy and the kids were there I could also forget that evening was coming, and with it the pain wave. But as they waved goodbye and I was wheeled inside, the long shadows over everything told it all, as if they were steadily eating away everything that was warm and comforting in my world until nothing was left but darkness, solitude, and agony.

I'd get wheeled back to my room knowing what was coming and wishing for all the world that it wouldn't.

For much of my time in Center Rehab the camera crew was still with me. They'd showed up two days after Thom had asked if it would be okay, and they were with me for two or three hours every day. They'd follow me everywhere: to HBO, to physical therapy, back to my room. And they'd interview me constantly. It started with Thom being there and just asking me questions about what I was feeling and thinking, and then became more of me explaining what was happening with my body and my healing as the weeks went on.

The best way to describe that whole part of the experience is "good and strange." I never got lonely having a camera operator, sound guy, and interviewer with me. I'm not sure it was easy for the medical staff to adjust to it (although they did), but what made it a little easier for me was that I knew all of those guys from work, and knew them well. Had they been strangers, things might have been much more awkward, and I might not have been as transparent as I was. In that way, having them there was a really good way for me to process through what was happening. I'm not good "in my head"; I always process verbally. They needed me to keep talking, and so by helping them I was also helping myself come to terms with everything.

The stranger part of it was that it took my mind off what I was going through, even while I was talking about what I was going through. Somehow, being able to focus my mind on telling the story of my ordeal separated me from it. Thom also had a knack for asking the kind of questions that would get me to give answers that gave some meaning to what was happening. Working with the film crew to set up shots, check lighting, and plan out scenes also made me feel like I was back in my old world, doing my old job, instead of just being the guy in the hospital bed.

Through it all, they saw the darker parts of it too. You'd think I would have put on a show, keeping it positive and light for the camera; but again, I knew these guys and it was very easy for me to just be myself. I wasn't self-conscious about being depressed or disappointed on camera. I really had no idea how they were going to use the footage, and without a preconceived vision about how things should turn out, there was nothing to influence how I let myself be portrayed. For me it was just a way to document that time of my life so that one day, when my kids were older, they could really know and understand what had happened.

At the time, neither Thom nor anybody else at Group really knew what all the footage would become either; there was just an undeniable belief that it should be done. And once again, it's impossible not to see the hand of God at work in it. In the end, the film crew and Group produced an incredible thirty-minute DVD and study guide designed to help people see how God can work through any situation to help us all have a deeper and growing relationship with Jesus. They called it *After the Fall* because of the tree that saved my life and led to the miracles that followed. In the same way, it was a tree that became the cross of Christ, who saved all of us and gave us miraculous new life. The leader's guide quotes 1 Corinthians 1:18, "The teaching about the cross is foolishness to those who are being lost, but to us who are being saved it is the power of God" (NCV). Those words could not have been more apt in describing the believer I was before the accident, and who I became.

In 2003, Group produced and distributed more than 50,000 copies of *After the Fall* at no charge to churches around the world. To this day, people still send me emails about it, and I hear, "Oh, you're *that* guy" at least once every other week. That video teaches me things even now, especially when I think back to the person I was while at Center Rehab.

For one, I was completely antisocial. I think if I have any regret about my time there, that's it, because what I'd started with the kid in the HBO room might have continued with other patients and staff at Center. Instead, I was focused on getting better and didn't need to be dragged down by interacting with people who had no hope of meaningful recovery. I even got the nurses to move me to the end of the hall because I was tired of being "plagued" by other residents just wandering in or simply staring in at me. It just made me nuts.

I know I was not the best example of Christian love. I still had this incredible new awareness of God, but that was just for *me* in my quiet times. Whenever someone was looking in at me or I had to do something that was painful or just humiliating, God was still relegated to second place. I regret that, but I can't take it back and, honestly, I don't believe God wants us to spend our lives regretting our mistakes. If we do, then the cross really means nothing. I learned from experience. I was (and am) still a work in progress. And in some ways, I really miss those days—not for my mistakes, but for those times when I set myself aside and really did get close to God.

The times when I was flat on my back, all alone, I could focus entirely on God. While Cyndy was taking the brunt of all the burdens my accident had thrust upon our family, I was free from the concerns and worries of regular life. All I had to focus on was getting better, and when I didn't focus on that, there was nothing to distract me from feeling God's calming presence. How many times have people been in the middle of prayer and suddenly wondered whether they'd paid the electric bill, or suddenly thought about work? As I recovered, there was none of that. There was nothing to distract or interrupt my thoughts as I prayed, I was able to focus on Him and give Him my entire mind and body. I had truly unfettered quiet time, where I could both pray and listen. God had gotten my attention, and He'd arranged things so He could keep it for a while.

I truly miss those days, and while I know I could have been a better Christian, it wasn't as if my time in Center didn't bear some fruit. I learned that Shelly and Dr. Lundy were both believers, and we'd often have wonderful talks about faith and God. I can't help but marvel about that; the two people God put most in charge of bringing me back were Christians. As they applied their skills and did all they could to physically repair me, they were also praying for me. And I know that's why, when it was time for me to leave Center Rehab thirteen weeks after I arrived, I was walking when I did it.

It was a slow process, getting on my feet again. Even as much as I wanted it to happen, I still had my doubts it *could* happen. My feet were just so busted up, I really had no idea if they could ever be up to the job of supporting me.

About two months after the accident, Shelly told me we were ready to start working our way up to walking again.

It started, like everything else, with the most basic movements. The wheelchair had foot rests on it and all I did at first was lift my feet off the rest and put them on the bare floor. I remember the sensation being a little weird, clunking my feet down with two casts on, and then working my foot in kind of a rolling motion. The casts had little rockers on them, and so to walk I'd have to learn to roll through the stepping motion. That was made all the more complicated by the general lack of feeling down there. My left foot could feel pressure here and there, but below my right knee I still had nothing. I still couldn't even wiggle my toes.

With my feet on the floor I'd start rocking my whole body forward, slowly but surely putting more weight on them, the goal being to eventually stand up.

I wasn't the only one worried about my feet holding together. I think my whole medical team gave in to a collective wince every time I put pressure on my feet, wondering whether or not they'd just explode all over again.

For better or worse, I'd lost a lot of weight. I've heard that when you go through heavy trauma like I had, your body just burns everything it can to help the healing process. Between that and the food, which was at best a chore to eat most of the time, almost thirty pounds of me disappeared. Considering that I was tipping a buck sixty-five when I came into the hospital, losing a quarter of my body weight in such a short time was a big deal. My doctors and the dieticians forced canned nutrition drinks on me. They'd bring two with every morning meal and, much as I needed something to wash the food down, that liquid chalk so deceptively labeled as a "shake" just didn't cut it. I decided to drink one and hide one, but with limited mobility and an acute lack of storage space, I couldn't get away with it for long. Cyndy and my parents became the shake police. They'd make me drink it in front of them. Ugh, it was awful.

I don't mean to disparage the product for what it does; there's no doubt it did its job keeping me nourished, but I think if I had to drink one now, or ever again, I'd puke.

All in all, the weight loss probably helped alleviate some of the concern about putting all of my weight on my feet. I progressed a little more each day until one afternoon, instead of our usual routine, Shelly brought me into a new room.

The first thing I noticed about this room was that it had parallel bars in it. Shelly put a thick belt around my waist and wheeled me over to the bars. The ends were just above eye level, two perfect circles. I was looking at them, wondering how this was going to work when, with one move, Shelly grabbed the belt and lifted me out of the chair. (Shelly's not exactly a petite thing, and in her line of work this was standard fare, but it was still impressive.) Once she had me out of the chair she brought me up to the bars and I placed a hand on each of them. My feet weren't touching the ground, I was stiff-armed and holding them a couple inches above the floor. Shelly held me around the waist and slowly lowered me, letting me gently put weight on my feet.

As she was holding me, it didn't hurt to stand up. And as she lowered me all the way, until all my weight was on my feet and I was basically supporting myself, I marveled all the more that it didn't hurt. Nothing I'd done with Shelly for the past several weeks had been without pain, so I just expected it, but miraculously with this there was none.

She asked me if I wanted to try walking. As much as I really, really did, I needed to rest a minute, so she sat me back down. I'd just gotten the emotional wind knocked out of me, and I needed a moment.

When I was ready, she hoisted me back onto the bars. I'd love to say I walked the length of them, but in truth it was more of me using the upper body strength I still had left to propel myself on stiff arms and drag my feet. My hips didn't work right—I couldn't rotate them yet—but knowing that, even so, I had enough upper body strength to hold myself up was important. That showed that at least I could use crutches to get around.

It was the first good news of this entire experience. I remember telling Cyndy about it and she cried tears of joy.

Real walking was still weeks away, but for the first time since the accident, I was moving on my own power. It was the first glimpse of the light at the end, the first time that everything seemed to be going in the right direction, and the first thing that told me my hopes and my faith were justified.

6

THE DIVINE MESSAGE OF HONEY NUT CHEERIOS

When it was time to leave Center Rehab, there was no threshold that had been crossed or milestone in my recovery that had at last been reached. My time had simply run out.

The human body heals itself to the best degree it can over the course of ten to thirteen weeks, and the big jumps occur in the first couple of months. The bones knit back together, the swelling subsides, and the scabs heal; and then you reach a point where you just can't scrape any more out of the bucket.

My foot flap had healed, but there was never a declaration that I'd cleared a hurdle and I was going to keep my foot. They told me there was no gangrene and no infection, but that only meant it wasn't going to have to come off right away. They basically put a stitch in it, called it good, and made a concerted effort to stay as vague as they possibly could about what the future might hold.

I still had to rely on a wheelchair, but I'd gotten remarkably good at walking around in casts with crutches or a walker. The casts were like giant plastic socks and they had a rocker on the bottom so I could walk a little more naturally. Even without feeling in my right foot I was pretty mobile. I just had to look down and see where the ground was to make sure my foot was actually on it.

From here on in it wouldn't be so much about healing, but adapting. That included dealing with the pain too; it was no longer about pain relief, but pain management. The pain would be a constant companion for the rest of my life, but with the right combination of therapies, medicines, and positive thinking, it wouldn't be debilitating. I'd already gotten beyond the point of shaking like a junkie as I waited for my meds. Things still really hurt, but I was free from the crippling kind of pain that made me want to puke. That was a blessing in itself.

A few days before I was officially released, I was reunited with the occupational therapist, who joined me and a physical therapist for a walk-through of my house. It was arranged for the middle of the day, at a time when no one would be there. They didn't want any distractions.

The house was eerie and quiet when I went in, which did little to calm the jitters I had about leaving the safe cocoon of the rehab center. We walked through every room in the house. Well, they walked. I could get around on a walker or crutches, but only for a short distance and then it was back into the wheelchair. It was amazing how big my house seemed after so long. I couldn't walk from end to end without wearing myself out.

As we went through the house, simulating what would be my everyday activities, my eyes at last were opened to what an important job the occupational therapist had. Her job was to help me figure out how I was going to do everything again.

I was simply amazed at how many stupid little things I had never thought about. Simple things that we all do without the slightest thought, like getting a bowl down from a shelf or just navigating a narrow doorway. Ordinary things, like opening a ground-level cabinet in a small bathroom—easy enough under ordinary circumstances, but a whole new perplexing problem if you're in a wheelchair and a back brace. I was amazed at how many things I'd have to relearn. They showed me how to get in and out of the shower, and they pinpointed where in the house we needed to install grab bars. They taught me how to navigate a wheelchair through the house without cratering the walls and to negotiate the narrow doorways without tearing all the trim off in the process. They told me I'd probably have to get a new bed, and something called a gravity chair, which would "unload my spine completely" and relieve the pressure in my back.

Most of all, they revealed the endless succession of booby traps in my own house that were conspiring to injure me. I'd never thought about the fact that hospitals don't have stairs, carpets, or small risers in narrow doorways. All these things were in my house, and any one of them was capable of snagging a crutch and sending me sprawling.

My feet and lower legs didn't have the strength or the feeling they'd need to kick out and rebalance me, so if something tripped me up, I was going down. Hard. And that would not be good for the hardware in my body or the chassis it was holding together.

I officially left for home on my thirty-eighth birthday in a mix of emotions. For almost eight weeks I'd been told by everyone with a medical degree that there'd be no more hiking, climbing, skiing, or anything else that might hit my right foot and cause a new injury. With that echoing in the back of my mind I was happy to be going home, but terrified of being on my own.

In the hospital everything was taken care of for me. I was sheltered and protected. I was led by doctors and nurses who controlled everything about my day, and who took care of every need. At home there would be no schedule, just me in two casts and a back brace with the kids running around, Cyndy still managing everything without any real help from me, and all of us in our own ways trying to come to terms with our new reality.

> **At home there would be no schedule, just me in two casts and a back brace with the kids running around, Cyndy still managing everything without any real help from me, and all of us in our own ways trying to come to terms with our new reality.**

The film crew was with us to document the glorious homecoming. They interviewed me in the morning, asking if I was excited and that sort of thing. None of them hinted at (nor was I thinking about) getting a warm reception from friends and family at the house. Even when one of them asked if he could keep me miked up for the ride home, it never occurred to me there might be an ulterior motive behind it.

As I was escorted outside for the last time, Cyndy pulled up in my pickup truck and everyone helped me climb in. The film crew jumped into their Suburban and drove on ahead.

Terrified as I was, however, it didn't take long to experience more of that "real joy" in the simplest and most mundane things. I rode home with the window down the whole time. It was a beautiful sunny day, and as I felt the warm air rushing over me, it was blissful. I then understood the joy every dog has when they stick their head out the car window and just breathe it all in. There's a lesson there for all of us.

As we topped a small rise and got a view of my house, I noticed the crowd. A welcoming party of twenty or thirty people, many of them co-workers, had gathered to celebrate my return home. They cheered and waved and threw streamers and gave me a hero's welcome with everything they had.

A million different things could have come to my mind at that moment. And from all those choices only one emerged.

I'm not wearing any pants.

I couldn't put pants on over the casts, so in the hospital I'd always just worn boxers. I'd gotten kind of used to it.

Fashion faux pas aside, the other unfortunate truth was that I just wasn't feeling too well physically. The ride in the truck had been a new kind of experience, and it was a little taxing. I'd expected that, and had really planned to just get home, take a few days to get into a rhythm and get my act together. Playing host right away was not part of the plan.

Still, I was really stunned by the outpouring of love and support. After all these people had done for me and for my family over the past two months, they had taken time out of their lives to greet me as I came home. The last thing I wanted was to come off acting like a jerk. I told myself to be a sport about it and, with as much energy as I could muster, I genuinely thanked them all so much for coming.

Cyndy had my walker ready, and I remember thinking what a drag it was to have to use a walker in front of everybody. Imagine that. Here's a guy alive, upright, and walking when by all laws of nature none of those things should be true, and he's embarrassed about using a walker in front of a crowd. The irony was not lost on me.

Mayah and Will ran up to the truck and climbed in to give hugs and kisses while Cyndy walked around the truck with my crutches. I could use them to get out of the car and up to the front porch, but as good as I was with them, I still couldn't use them to get up stairs. Hence the walker. I was feeling a mixture of emotions as I took the crutches in hand, eased out of the truck, and made my way to the front porch.

Not counting the visit with the therapists, fifty-four days had passed since the last time I had crossed the threshold of my own house. Doing it again was no picnic; negotiating the small rise at the bottom of the door required a little bit of a slow dance move, but I pulled it off and then just collapsed into a chair.

I didn't know if everyone was going to follow us inside, where there'd be food refreshments and a little party, but I did know that despite my earlier decision to knuckle up and show some gratitude, I really wasn't up to it. I was too wiped to even dwell on it. Fortunately, Cyndy must have given everyone a heads-up in advance that it was too early for me to be very social, because other than cheering and welcoming me home, no one made a move to come inside. They were all very cool and very respectful about it. Cyndy simply thanked everyone for coming and waved goodbye as she gently closed the door.

And then my family and I were all alone in the house. I was home. And I really had no idea what was supposed to happen next.

Cyndy and I didn't talk too much. She just let me know that if there was anything I needed, I only had to ask. I didn't even know what to ask for. The body I missed was gone forever, and I had to take stock of what was left. It seemed like a short list.

Looking around the house, it seemed like I had been gone for years. I hadn't been in my own house in so long that I'd forgotten what it smelled like; that pleasant mixture of kids and cooking and pets and coffee had been all but lost to me. I knew every nook and cranny of the place, yet it just didn't feel familiar.

But as I settled in, the old familiarity began to come back. It brought with it a warm rush of joy at being home again at last. But it also brought a reminder that my old life was gone forever, and warned that my new life was going to reveal itself to me in a long series of pleasant and unpleasant discoveries.

That first night, as I lay in my own bed again at last, grateful to have Cyndy beside me once more, I heard the heater click on. It was a sound so distinctly "my house." It was something I'd heard a thousand times before as I was drifting off to sleep and as I heard it, it was as if that missing "something" had finally been put back into place. In that instant I felt suddenly normal. It was just another early autumn night at chez DeMartino and it was almost as if the horror of the accident and my recovery had never happened.

Beyond that one moment, however, my first night home was miserable. My bed was no hospital bed. It didn't adjust up or down, it was just a flat mattress and my sleep was constantly interrupted by the strangeness of the bed and the fact that I couldn't get comfortable.

I also woke up the next day in a boatload of pain. I knew I was going to spend the day stacking meds trying to catch up with it. There are much better ways to start a day.

Of course, that first morning also brought the first breakfast with my kids in two months and, equally important, reunited me with Honey Nut Cheerios.

I'd always liked them, but I'd forgotten how much. It had also been a long time since I had enjoyed a bowl of them in my own kitchen, with my own milk, at my own table. It was suddenly so apparent how lucky I'd been and how incredible it was that I was home. It was another powerful reminder of the million little blessings that flow through our lives every day that we otherwise never notice. Nothing had ever tasted so good in my life. I ate two bowls.

The camera crew caught it all, and they were quite amused. I confess I *had* taken a healthy dose of pain meds before wheeling into the kitchen that morning. I can see why they started chuckling as I looked at the camera, spoon in hand, and proclaimed: "these are soooo *good!*"

As powerful as my feelings of thanks were for being home, what was hardest to take was that God seemed to have gone quiet.

My whole overarching feeling in coming home could be stated as *okay, I've come out of this big thing . . . I've had this big epiphany, and through all the interviews and public attention—where I'd talked more about my faith in a few weeks than I had in all the previous years—it's become clear that God was steering me to leave rehab because something was going to happen.*

If I could boil it down to a word, it would be *expectation*. I just had this feeling God had been opening doors for me specifically so He could lead me somewhere. And then I got home and I suddenly felt completely alone. It was as if God had simply seen me through the worst of it only to say, "Okay, bye!" and leave.

I remember praying, *God, it's very clear what You said to me two months ago, but now I'm home with no future and no idea what normal is, and You're silent.*

Fifty times a day I would thank God for keeping me alive. For helping me recover as much as I had. For getting me home, where I wanted to be. And I could see His grace everywhere, especially in the friends who would bring dinner, visit, and send cards. I saw the beauty of how God's people connected and pulled together.

But as the weeks went on, the apparent absence of God became like a huge hole. I kept thinking God would keep guiding me, and He wasn't. Where I should have seen His hand at work all around me, instead almost every experience was a muddled collage of good and bad, as if joy and despair were waging war inside me, and to the victor would go my spirits.

Where I should have seen His hand at work all around me, instead almost every experience was a muddled collage of good and bad, as if joy and despair were waging war inside me, and to the victor would go my spirits.

Each day would have its precious moments, and I cherished every one of them. When it was time for Mayah to go to sleep I could lie on her bed and talk with her. Just hearing that sweet little girl voice as the shadows lengthened would make me the happiest man on earth. But I couldn't pick her up. She couldn't even snuggle against me because of the back brace. The first time she tried, she banged her head against it. She wasn't hurt, but the ensuing "ouch" was like a knife. These kids had been through so much in the last two months; now they finally had their dad back and I couldn't even comfort them at bedtime.

I couldn't play with them either, at least not in the rough and tumble, wrestling way that dads are supposed to play with their kids sometimes. My first few weeks I was at home I felt incredibly vulnerable, especially to the kids, who basically had to be told, "Don't break Daddy . . ."

At other times, I could just sit with the kids in my new zero-gravity chair where I'd read to them and be so grateful that there was no reason for me to have to be moved someplace else, and no need for them to leave after only a couple hours.

I began to embrace the fact that I could create my own patterns rather than have them prescribed for me. I still had to schedule my life—our lives—around doctor and physical therapy appointments but even those were at times Cyndy and I chose. It was quite empowering.

Once I established a new habit of wheelchairing into the kitchen and waiting for that morning's pain meds to kick in, even that part of the day became comforting. I was getting into a rhythm of my own choosing. I was getting back in control of my life. If I wanted go outside and sit in the warm summer sun, I could just wheel myself out onto the patio and soak up some of the vitamin D my now pale and emaciated body so desperately needed. Every time I did, I would marvel at the beauty of fall in Colorado. That would start me really thinking about photography again. Getting my head back into old patterns of thinking was an incredibly welcome change.

I'd also take great joy in accompanying Maya to the movies, sitting in the stands with Cyndy at the kids' soccer games and going out for pizza afterward, and the million other things I was doing, despite the fact that I should have been dead, or at least paralyzed and trapped in a body that couldn't work.

But spiritually and emotionally there was this gaping hole where the only thing I could count on feeling was pain. Beyond that I had no focus or feeling of purpose.

That experience even became evident in my prayer time. In the hospital I'd been able to shut everything else out and let my prayers be pure, untroubled, and uninterrupted. In my house, it was like some kind of plug had been pulled. That genuine closeness with God felt somehow obstructed.

It was a very awkward and uncomfortable feeling, and a strange time in my life. I had no compass. I was meandering through a day-to-day existence waiting for something to happen while Cyndy was still picking up all the slack in our lives and emotionally trying to figure me out. As the holidays came around, I was stuck in a weird and frustrating rut. I was trying to fit back into the mold of my old life, but the constant reminders that I never would (reminders which usually came courtesy of my leg) just became maddening.

The thought that I might have to give up on my leg remained an unacceptable one. No one was willing to tell me that my right leg had to come off yet, but the continued lack of feeling was not an encouraging sign. I think the people around me, and maybe even God too in His own way, wanted me to start thinking about the positive side of losing my leg, but I was nowhere near ready for that. I knew that for sure when a friend came by to visit one day. He'd lost his leg years before and he wanted to show me his prosthesis.

He had been and still was a very active person, so I listened to him, or pretended to, and tried to be convincing when I told him that I would think about things a little more. But when he took that fake leg off and rested that stump on my bed I almost jumped out of my skin. Honestly, it was all I could do to just not recoil from it. It was abhorrent; and here was this guy showing me this thing as if doing so would make me decide I wanted to be like him. No. No way.

I'd wanted to believe the casts, the crutches, and all the rest of it were just temporary. I figured that since God had been there for me in the hospital in such a powerful way that He would continue to heal me. To make me whole. I even said in one interview that God was listening to me.

It was Dr. Lundy who had to tell me I'd likely wear a walking cast on my lower right leg for the rest of my life. I didn't want to accept that. I tried to put a shoe on that foot and walk, but the pain of that made it impossible. I had a custom cast made for my foot, but I couldn't convince even myself that it looked natural.

I kept thinking, *Wow, this is it. I really need some guidance and direction here.* In the hospital I'd sensed God's hand, but now that I was back in the world I was feeling a little lost. You'd think someone who'd been through everything I had in the past few months would have noticed God's hand in everything going on around me, but it was still months before I even got a clue.

I remember the day. It was about a month after I'd come home, long after I'd realized how weak my faith was, and how God was reaching out to me. I was feeling sorry for myself, and I asked the inevitable question of Cyndy, "Why would God let this happen to me?"

"God didn't let this happen," she said. "This was human error. Two men made mistakes, and from the second you left that ledge God has been there for you, for me, for all of us. He has taken over everything to guide us, heal you, and move us forward."

I didn't know how I could have been so blind. Only after she said that were my eyes finally opened to the string of miracles that had gotten me off the mountain, gotten me to the hospital, and surrounded me with doctors and therapists who, in the course of doing their jobs, would shut the door to my room and pray with me.

It was about then I also started to really understand what Cyndy had been going through, mostly alone.

Around me, Cyndy had always been amazing. Her attitude was always one of support and strength. When I was in the hospital and it had seemed like all was lost, I'd look up and the person standing there was my wife. To this day I wonder, if she had been the one who'd gotten hurt, would I have been half as strong as she was? I could see the physical toll it was taking on her—having a busted up husband and having to live the life of a single mom. I could see it on her face, in her eyes, and I could hear it in her voice. But she never said a word of complaint.

As bad as everything was for me while I was in the hospital and rehab, for Cyndy it had been much worse. At the end of every day I had the pain meds and the promise of sleep. For Cyndy there was no respite. The nightmare just went on.

The story of the accident and what happened afterward was never just mine, and it can't be honestly or completely told without Cyndy's voice. I could never do justice to her struggle or her strength by simply telling the world what I thought she was feeling and experiencing, or even by repeating what she told me. That part of the story must be told from her perspective, and in her own words.

7

CYNDY'S STORY

On the day the call came I wasn't thinking about how much our lives would change. I never even thought I'd get that kind of phone call. Those calls came to other people, other homes, and other wives.

We'd had friends of friends who knew someone who'd been hurt climbing, but it had never hit close to home. Accidents didn't happen to people with as much experience as Craig; that was how my mind characterized the risk. We'd never even really talked about what to do if either one of us had a serious climbing accident, although on one occasion when we were ice climbing together, miles from any help, I did say that if something happened I needed to know where the car keys were. He just laughed and said, "Oh, nice!" and that was about how much we dwelt on those thoughts. Of course we had life insurance, just in case, but couples in their mid-thirties never think about needing it. It's too easy to think you're invincible.

Even as the helicopter lifted off, carrying Craig to the hospital, I had no idea what was coming. Nor did I have any idea what all it would teach me. About forgiveness, especially for myself. About grace, about friendship, about compassion. About how much we need God in our lives, and that we don't need to wait for something horrible to happen, or until there's nothing else left, because God is there for us all the time and we should just go to Him first.

As I plunged head over heels into the darkest period of my life, it was easy to miss the miracles and blessings all around me. My focus was never able to get that wide, but looking back there's no question—God carried me and our family through this in just the same way He carried Craig off that mountain.

But before I could begin to understand that, I would spend months as an emotional wreck. I was glad Craig was alive, but everything about the future was an unknown. I had to face some terrifying questions.

What if Craig couldn't walk again? What if he lost his legs? What if he was paralyzed? What if he couldn't work again? Craig had been the breadwinner while I stayed home with Mayah and Will. The possibility he wouldn't work again, and what that would mean for all of us, weighed terribly on me. The questions just went on and on, and as bad as the questions were, the lack of any answers made everything worse.

I also had to take on a role as Craig's health care case manager. He had an orthopedic surgeon, a neurosurgeon, and a host of other doctors looking in on him, but they all dealt with individual parts of his body. No one was taking on the job of looking at him as a whole person or managing his overall care, so I had to. I had to advocate for his care both in the hospital and with the insurance companies, and I was a blind person stumbling through the health care system. Even with the invaluable assistance I got from an HR commando at Craig's work, who truly did the lion's share of navigating through the health care maze, I still had to spend hours on the phone arguing and freaking out over what would be covered and what wouldn't. When Craig had to leave the hospital for a rehab center I needed to find a place that offered the kind of care a man his age needed and insurance would pay for. The hospital had staff that helped me, but it was another layer of pressure and stress. And every moment of it all was time away from Craig, and time I wasn't being a mom for our kids.

That was probably hardest on me. The kids didn't ask a lot of questions about where Daddy was—they were more concerned with when he was coming home. They came with me every day and knew he was in the hospital, but they were distraught and displaced; their lives were turned upside down. As a stay-at-home mom I'd been there with them and for them 24-7 before the accident. Suddenly Daddy was gone all the time, and I was gone at least half the time. It was a difficult rhythm. The kids missed him, and they missed "us." When they had to leave the hospital and go home with Craig's parents while I stayed behind they would cry, unable to understand why they couldn't stay too. And when I joined them at home later there'd be more tears that Daddy wasn't with me. They missed him so much. They asked me every day when he'd get home. I told them the truth, that I didn't know, but the doctors were doing the best they could and it was going to take time. I was trying to be rational with a one- and a three-year-old. That went about as well as anyone would expect.

Being gone so much also affected my ability as a parent. The kids were acting out and trying my patience in the extreme, and I was so emotionally drained and depressed from not knowing how we were going to make it through this that even when I was with them it was hard to be the mom they so desperately needed. It's hard enough to be a parent to a one- and three-year-old, but in the middle of all this crisis, I was just trying to cope myself. To try to be a mom at all, much less a good one, was often more than I could handle. I know a lot of people do it, but for me it was really a struggle. Everything I had wasn't enough, and there was nowhere else to dig.

All the kids wanted was their mom and dad, but they weren't getting either and they were too young to understand or deal with what they were feeling. When they couldn't get the attention they needed, they'd act out more, and not just with me. I remember one Sunday after church when I went to pick Mayah up from Sunday school, the teacher took me aside. Mayah had really been at it that morning, disrupting class, refusing to listen or behave and just causing problems. The teacher had to tell me that if Mayah couldn't behave and be a better listener, she couldn't keep coming back.

I pretty much just burst into tears. Here was one more thing I couldn't handle. And if my daughter was being kicked out of Sunday school, I couldn't come to church. I already had too many "what am I going to do then?" questions suffocating me. I didn't need one more.

We were fairly new to that church at the time and the teacher didn't know what had been going on with us. Fortunately another teacher in the class did know our story and defused the whole situation, but it was more evidence, in my mind, of how I was failing my kids.

In one of the few times I tried to do something normal I took them to Dairy Queen for ice cream. Mayah, being three, accidentally spilled hers. It should have been no big deal, but I'd been under too much stress for too long. All the frustration and emotional trauma I'd been bottling up came out and I read Mayah the riot act. I put her in her car seat a little rougher than usual, hollering at her the whole time about how she needed to be more careful. Then she said something I'll never forget for the rest of my life.

"Mom, God is so mad at you right now."

I just stopped and looked at her, and tears filled my eyes. Everything about the kind of parent I'd been for the past two months had just been called out on the mat. I knew what kind of mom I'd been, but now Mayah knew it too. It rocked me to my core. I felt like the worst sinner, and the worst parent in the universe. The guilt was overwhelming.

"You are so right," I told her through a sob, trying to pull myself together and knowing I had to do better.

After that I continued to spend a lot of time in prayer and in tears. I carried guilt around for a long time. With that, on top of everything else, I became really depressed. Emotionally I went down to places I'd never been before. There were times I prayed for God to take my life. Let me be in a car accident on the way home so I don't have to do this anymore. I couldn't deal with the stress and the sadness and the thousand terrifying questions about the future that couldn't be answered. There was never a day off. It was too much.

For months, my whole life was consumed by stress, worry, fear, sleep deprivation, and worst of all, anger. For the longest time, as much as I loved him and prayed for him and wanted him to get better, I was really angry at Craig.

It didn't come on right away. It was more like it grew and evolved the more I talked with him after the accident and we began piecing together what happened. As I learned more about who had said what and when, I couldn't believe what I was hearing.

I finally asked Craig why he had asked Steve to take him off belay, and why he had skipped yelling "on belay" before he started down. In my mind, I was thinking that's basic climbing procedure. Really, *it's the first thing you learn.*

Craig answered me honestly, but it was hard to be satisfied with "I screwed up," and the more I thought about it, the angrier I got. This wasn't a little mistake that could be shrugged off. He took a shortcut, didn't follow protocol, and it had cost all of us dearly.

There were times I wanted to scream, *How could you do this to us?* To our dreams and our plans for the future? Part of climbing is taking all kinds of precautions—how could he have skipped those? He knew better. And now his mistake was going to change our lives forever, in who knew how many ways. All the stress I was under, trying to be a mom, a wife, a caregiver, and Craig's health care manager—punctuated by nights of crying myself to sleep—it was all because he hadn't done what he knew he was supposed to.

You'd think I'd have been angry at Steve too, but I wasn't. As I saw it, it was Craig's life that had been on the line, so it was Craig's responsibility to make sure his belayer had him secure.

Angry as I was, I knew that anger wasn't something I could express to Craig. I just bottled it in, and it grew and grew until it was too much of a struggle for me to control it, and in a weak and tired moment I said something I wished I hadn't. I don't even remember what we were talking about. It was at a time we were both feeling the grief of what our lives had become. Before I knew it, the words were out.

"If you had just done things the way you should have, this wouldn't have happened."

I hadn't yelled, but the tone didn't matter. Craig just looked at me, and I knew I could never go there again. The look on his face . . . It wasn't that he was angry. It was more like he was so beaten down already that he couldn't handle having me mad at him too. I knew he was dealing with his own guilt for everything we were going through and he was giving everything he had to get better and get us past this. He didn't need my blame on top of that.

As I left the hospital that day, I piled an extra load of guilt onto my emotional train wreck. I was losing my ability, and my will, to hold it all together. I knew I had to find a way to get past this anger or we were going to be in real trouble.

Some people ask me if I ever thought about divorcing Craig or just leaving him, but that was the furthest thing from my mind. I still loved him deeply. It was the situation that I wanted to be out of, not my marriage. I was just angry at what he'd done. Nonetheless, it's pretty easy for me to see why, when someone suffers a traumatic injury, it splits couples apart. It can be hard enough if a marriage facing typical obstacles is on rocky ground, but in a situation like this it's like suddenly two people can't identify or help with what the other is going through. Add a whole bunch of pain, depression, and anger on top of that, and even the best marriages will struggle. I've heard of couples ripped apart because someone's in so much pain that they constantly have to be medicated and are never the same again. It wasn't like that for us. We could still see each other and talk together, and I was incredibly thankful for that. In accidents like Craig's, head injuries and brain damage are pretty common, but he had none of that. How that's even possible I don't know. God put that tree there and when Craig hit it, I think it saved him. He was badly hurt, but he could still think and talk and be present the same way he always had. We could still talk about what was happening, what decisions we had to make, and carry the load together as a couple. I still had my best friend. If I hadn't, I don't know if I could have made it.

As much as we talked, I tried not to share too much of my own struggles with Craig when we were together. He had so many of his own. I didn't want him to be burdened with mine at all. I kept a lot of what I was going through to myself, and asked God to put in over-time, because He was all I had. I could only ask so much of our friends and family, and they had all stepped up in the extreme—I was by no means left on my own.

When Craig's parents heard about the accident they came out right away. They dropped everything and stayed at our house for a month. They were so gracious and they provided a ton of support. As much as I felt like I wasn't doing a good job on any front, what little I was doing would have been impossible without them. After that my mom came out and helped for a little while as well, and our friends and neighbors were a constant blessing, from the friend who randomly came and mowed our lawn, and the eighty-year-old neighbor who trimmed our hedges when by all respects we should have been trimming his, to the friends and neighbors who brought us meals, to Craig Luben, who organized fundraisers for us, and Craig's co-workers, who donated their vacation time so we could have a paycheck while he was recovering.

And I had close friends available when I just needed to talk, but no one I knew had a frame of reference for what we were going through. In parenting, a lot of times you can turn to friends and ask what they'd do in certain kinds of kid-raising situations, but this was so far off the radar there was nothing they could do to help me, and there came a time when I just couldn't do it anymore. It was draining on them, and knowing that was draining me. I felt like they didn't need to hear about the next worse thing—almost every day while Craig was in the hospital it seemed like there was more bad news. I didn't want to bur-den them anymore. Right or wrong, that's how I felt. I had to rely on

God or I wasn't going to make it. Sometimes it went okay. Sometimes it didn't. I prayed for God's forgiveness and guidance if I didn't handle something well, and I prayed for wisdom and patience to be a better parent and not be yelling at my kids all the time. I felt like I was so low that only God could help me. He was all I had. And I knew He was there for me.

I finally decided to see a counselor. I remember for the first few sessions it seemed like all I could do was cry.

Before the accident, I was already having a tough time. I was still grieving the loss of my father, who had been killed in a work accident the previous year. He owned an ice company that he'd built up himself. He was a super smart guy and I dearly loved and respected him. They were moving a huge tractor/trailer-sized icebox and my dad, who was alongside it, was crushed when the jack fell out. He died instantly. He had just told one of his employees to get out of the way in case the jack slipped, probably saving that man's life, but for whatever reason my dad chose to stay in harm's way. He made a mistake and it cost him his life.

When I told the counselor that, she stopped me and asked a question. "Aren't you angry at your dad?"

"No," I told her. "It was just an accident."

When I told her that, I suddenly had a whole new perspective on what had happened with Craig. It was one of those "whoa . . ." moments as I was sitting there in her office. Yes, Craig had made mistakes, but he and Steve had had very different perceptions of what they were saying to each other. I could see how it had happened, and I could finally understand it. What had happened was an accident. A horrible one, but not one I should blame him for.

As I left the counselor's office, I let things roll around in my head. I thought and thought and thought. I thought about how God had forgiven me for all my mistakes—mistakes I'd made on a daily basis. I took a hard look at myself and the anger I'd been harboring and I thought, *How can I think that way? Who am I to be this angry? Look at how many mistakes I make every day, look at how I sin every day, and God forgives me every time.*

It was an incredibly powerful lesson for me. I realized the way I was handling this was so much worse than anything Craig had done. I needed to forgive him, and I needed to let the anger go.

I wouldn't have thought that after months and months of teeth-grinding frustration, anger, and stress, I could just blink and it would all be gone, but that's exactly what happened. I was suddenly free. Even at the time, I couldn't believe it was gone so quickly, but there was no denying how I felt. I felt *better*. The problems didn't go away and there was still plenty of stress and worry and bad news to deal with. I was still emotionally raw, and I continued to make mistakes and handle things poorly. I still would pray, desperately, for God to get me through the next hour, or the rest of the afternoon. There was even still anger from time to time, but it wasn't the deep-rooted anger that could stoke every tense moment into something worse. I had a new perspective, and with it I could get back, emotionally, to where I needed to be.

Part of that meant coming to terms with the very real possibility that Craig and I would never climb together again. Selfish and shallow as it sounds, it was a huge loss for me to think about that. The doctors were telling me that it was probably over for Craig in many ways. No more walking. No more climbing. All the things we loved.

A lot of people might be surprised at my wanting him to climb again instead of absolutely forbidding it. I mean, it had almost killed him. And maybe if I wasn't a climber as well that's how it would have been but, like Craig, I'd fallen in love with the sport, and in much the same way he had.

Growing up I was not an athlete. I didn't play team sports, so I didn't really fit in. When I found climbing, it was something I was good at, and to finally find a sport I could excel in brought me a lot of joy. There's not another sport I've ever tried that provides the kind of fulfillment that climbing does. It's the flow of the movement, almost gymnastic-like sometimes, and ballet-like at others. It's the mental challenge. There's the slight

twinge of fear in it, and forcing myself not to let the fear stop me from moving on. To have fear, to know it's there, and yet be able to harness it and succeed in something you at first think maybe you can't do, is empowering in a way I've never felt in anything else.

> To have fear, to know it's there, and yet be able to harness it and succeed in something you at first think maybe you can't do, is empowering.

Being in God's creation that way was also a huge spiritual thing for me—to be in these beautiful places I'd have never otherwise seen if not for climbing. Sharing that with my husband made it something very special.

That experience was something Craig and I both understood and felt together. I think that shared passion for the sport also helped us forge a really strong marriage. When you climb with someone, you get to know them pretty well. There are plenty of high stress situations to work through, and who you really are comes out when you climb together. You're also forced to work together, to rely on each other, and take comfort in knowing your partner is there and has your back. You have to trust each other with your very lives. That forged an incredibly strong bond between us and made it easier to work things out in all the other parts of our lives. Craig and I rarely ever fought, and even when we disagreed on something or were just in a mood, climbing was our common ground. He told me once that no matter what happened between the two of us, we could always return to climbing and be on the same page.

Climbing wasn't just something the two of us shared alone either. Before the kids came we'd go ice climbing on the weekends, climbing all day and camping at night. We continued climbing together even after the kids, just in more family-friendly places. We shared a passion for climbing with our circle of friends. Climbing together, encouraging each other and celebrating the joys of it together, was a cornerstone of our lives. And it broke my heart to think it might be gone.

I really questioned what we were going to do as a couple if we couldn't climb together anymore. I knew we could still experience God's creation just going for a drive, but that didn't offer anything close to the kind of fulfillment climbing did. Even if Craig could climb again someday, I had no way of knowing *if* he would. If it was not going to be a source of joy for him anymore, which I could completely understand, then I was going to have to accept that. I was never going to push him back into it and I didn't want him to feel like he was obligated to go back to climbing just for me. He needed to want to come back to it on his own, on his own terms.

I was probably too focused on that at the time to really understand that even if he never climbed again, that was okay, because we would always have our common faith to unite us. I didn't know it at first, but we were both growing in our faith together, even though we were each experiencing it in our own individual ways.

Before the accident I was a lot like Craig in terms of my faith—a believer, but not someone who put a lot of thought into needing God. That changed pretty fast. I had no idea how difficult it would be for me to find the strength to get our family through this. I had no plan for how to be a mom, a wife, and Craig's health care advocate all at once. There were times I didn't know how I was going to get through the next hour, never mind the next day or next week or next month with no end in sight. I finally got to a place where I had to realize I couldn't do it on my own. If I tried, I wasn't going to make it. I needed God's help in a way I'd never experienced before. I had to rely on Him to give me what I needed to carry on, whether it was a call from a friend, a moment's peace, or even just a feeling of comfort. I put all my trust in my faith, knowing that if I did, God would see me through.

When Craig had his discovery in the hospital about his own faith, what was remarkable was that we both came to the same place, spiritually. He came to that place through inspiration, I came by necessity, but we both still got there. We both realized we'd been treating God like an accessory, and God used the accident to bring us closer to Him, each in our own way. He probably knew I would never have had the same kind of experience Craig did by reading a book. I'm more of a "learn things the hard way" kind of girl. God knew that, and put me through the hardest time of my life. Not to whip me into shape, but to show me how much I needed Him, to draw me closer to Him, and to grow me in my faith.

As much as we all wanted and waited and wished for Craig to come home, when the time finally came I was not prepared for it. I was even a little fearful. I had no idea how I was supposed to care for him. He came home with a full neck brace, back brace, and two walking casts. I had no help if Craig needed assistance getting around. We'd talked a little bit about it with his occupational therapist, but there are thousands of little things we do that we take for granted every day, and talking about things was no real substitute for actually knowing what to do. I'm a strong girl, but I didn't even know how I was going to get him out of the car when we got home. I didn't know what I was going to do if he needed me to get him to the shower, or the bathroom, or from the bed to a chair, or get him around town, much less do all that and keep taking care of two little kids.

He was still pretty fragile too, and I had liked the fact that he had twenty-four-hour care at the hospital and the rehab center. But at home, what was I supposed to do if he fell and got hurt somewhere in the house? I was really concerned about having to take on the job of being his nurse. He was going from constant professional medical attention and care to none.

It was all needless worry. From the moment we pulled up to the house and Craig got out of the car, waving to the crowd of friends who'd come to cheer his return and walking on his own power, I knew things were going to work out. God provided. Between his casts and his wheelchair Craig could be pretty self-sufficient, and before long he could even drive himself to his appointments. We also had a little bit of home health care once a week. It was little things, but it was enough.

And the kids just adored having him home at last. There was still a lot he couldn't do with them, but it meant a lot to all of us that he could be present in the kids' lives again. It just meant making an adjustment. He couldn't wrestle or run around with them or push them on the swings, but that didn't matter because the things he could do were the most meaningful. He could snuggle up with them. He could hold them in his lap and read them a story. He could give them his quiet and gentle attention, and that was what they needed most. It was a good change, and it turned out that having him home was easier on me, despite my earlier concerns. Having him home actually solved some problems. Gone were the days of coordinating schedules and pickups and logistics so kids could be watched while I stayed at the hospital. It was much easier to manage the kids' needs, and Craig's, when we were all in one place.

Of course, Craig couldn't mow the lawn or shovel snow or take care of all the household chores that he used to, but that didn't stop him from wanting to as his strength came back. I never told him "no" when he wanted to do something—I wanted to be his wife, not his mother. I did insist he choose wisely though, because we both knew that any time he overexerted himself, he was going to pay for it the next day. Instead, there could be tradeoffs. If he didn't mow the lawn one day and let me do it instead, that meant he could have more time with the kids tomorrow. Sometimes that really meant stopping him from rushing into something. I know he didn't like it. Doing all those kinds of chores meant a lot in terms of getting back to normal. He wanted to be himself again, to be more than just present. It made him feel more like himself to be participating in what was going on with the house and the kids.

He was still in a lot of pain too. It was nowhere near what he'd experienced in the early days at the hospital, but even on his best days he was still managing pain instead of being free from it. He rarely let it show though. Craig's attitude has always been one of the things I admire most about him. He's always positive—not in a naïve and illogical way, but just in a hope-giving way that comes with knowing what he can do if he puts his mind to it. Even before the accident, when we'd be climbing together, his supportive attitude would help get me through a tough spot. "You have to say you can do this," he'd always tell me when a really tricky part of a climb was coming up. Looking back, I can see so many parallels between the sport Craig and I loved so much and his approach to recovery that it's hard not to see God giving him a passion for climbing just so he could be prepared for life after the accident. His positive attitude did as much to get me through those really horrible times as it did for him. He made it possible for us as a couple to get through this. I rarely saw him cry, and I know he went through some really tough stuff. He just has this outlook that's so uplifting; he knows how to look at things from the bright side, from the side of hope and laughter. He told himself he had to get out of bed, and he would. He told himself he had to walk around the block, and he would. He told himself he had to go back to work, and he did.

Truthfully, there was no choice. He had to go back to work. The insurance and donated vacation hours were running out, and disability wasn't an option. For one, it only covered a fraction of his paycheck. For two, Craig didn't want to be disabled. Spending the rest of his life on the couch and unable to provide for his family just wasn't his style.

We did talk about me going back to work, and I was willing, but we had to be pragmatic. We'd gotten married almost right after I graduated from college with a wildlife biology degree, and had Mayah pretty soon after that. I wasn't established in a career like Craig was. My only options were entry-level jobs that simply wouldn't pay enough for us to live on. There was no getting around it—Craig needed to go back to work or we were going to hit a pretty serious financial wall.

After a few weeks at home Craig said he was ready. I didn't try to dissuade him, but quietly I thought he was going back prematurely. He'd go in for half days and come home exhausted and in so much pain that it was hard to watch. It took everything he had to be able to do even that much in those first few weeks, but neither of us knew what else we could do.

As the weeks went on, Craig got stronger and working became easier. His boss and his co-workers went above and beyond to accommodate him—they showed us so much grace—and in time there was no longer a question about Craig's ability to work or earn an income. We slowly started to settle into a new routine and a new life. I came around to the realization that in addition to letting go of the anger, I also needed to let go of the guilt I'd been carrying, especially when it came to the kids. I was thankful they were so young and that there was so much they wouldn't remember. Because of that it was better to focus on how I could be a good parent going forward instead of hating myself for the mistakes I'd made in the past.

As a family, together, we moved steadily out of crisis mode, knowing we should keep turning to God and staying close to Him even as things got better. And I'm glad we did, because crisis mode only went on pause. There were still more dark days ahead.

8

THE CUT

When I asked God to heal me, I wasn't very specific.

Look at almost any Bible study or devotional that talks about how to pray and the most common advice is: "Be specific." You wouldn't go into a car dealer and just ask for a car; you'd ask for a model, year, color, interior . . . everything down to the floor mats.

There's a comedian who once referred to ambiguity as "the devil's volleyball." All theology aside, there's a lot of wisdom in that little joke. My just asking God to "heal me" was like walking onto a lot and asking for a car.

Life became a very gradual uphill climb after coming home. I use that analogy on purpose; I'm no stranger to gradual climbs but the kind I was used to always had an end that was somewhere tangibly in sight. For this climb back to health, I'd keep going as much as I could, but the summit wouldn't be so much an achievement as it would be the point at which my body said "this far and no more." I had no idea where that would be.

The breakthroughs were smaller, fewer, and farther between as the focus moved away from physical healing and more into coping mechanisms. I had to figure out how this new body was going to work and how, within those dimensions, I was going to relate to my wife and kids and neighbors and a world that was so set in its own rhythms that I had little choice but to try to keep up.

I was trapped in a pit, feeling like I had no purpose.

And I did my best, but I was trapped in a pit, feeling like I had no purpose. I was reclaiming my role as a dad and husband, but not in the way I had hoped. And the other huge facets of my identity, work and climbing, were nothing close to certain. I wasn't ready to accept what life would be like without those things. It's not that I was in denial, it was just that I truly had no idea what life would be like without them. I was lost, without the first idea of how to even start charting a new course.

It was plainly evident that God was at work in the amazing community of believers that surrounded us at this time. People were dropping off food and well wishes at the house daily, and they did that for months. It was both crazy and humbling.

Then at last, someone threw a rope into the pit.

Then at last, someone threw a rope into the pit.

Almost from the day I came home, Bill came over a couple times a week with all the latest stories about what was going on at work. He's the art director at Group, so after catching up on a little bit of gossip we'd inevitably settle into talking shop and brainstorming ideas. It was pure milk and honey for my brain and my spirits. Just having normal conversations again and getting back to the things my brain knew about was both uplifting and calming.

After I'd been home a few weeks, Bill came to me one day and asked for my help.

"We've got a photo shoot we need to do at a park nearby, and I just don't want to trust this to the intern," he said. "There are lots of nice flat paved walkways. I can push you in your chair if I need to, but I'd like you to do this one."

I was still on short-term disability and didn't have to return to work, but that free ride was heading quickly toward a hard stop and I'd have to go back to work before the insurance ran out. That reality, as significant as it was, was not really the reason I told Bill yes. The truth was I knew I needed to try to figure out how I was going to reclaim my work identity, and this would be a good first test. To this day I still wonder if Bill knew that all along.

That day turned out to be a big day of firsts for me. It was the first time I drove since the accident and it was just good to know that I could have that freedom of mobility, back brace and all. Bill did have to push me in the chair. I had crutches with me but I could only stand for a couple minutes before I'd have to sit right back down. But when it came to composing and framing the shots, letting my eyes do their job, and working the camera, it all came together. It wasn't as automatic as it had been. Shooting from a sitting position isn't like shooting from a standing position, but overall it was an incredible leap forward for me. At last I had a sense of how things could work. I could see everything piecing together . . . eventually I was going to be able to reclaim my life as a photographer, and a provider for my family, after all.

From that day I steadily eased back into work. I'd been really nervous about making the transition to the office again, but I was immediately put at ease by an immeasurable amount of support and understanding from Thom and everyone at Group who told me "just do what you can and we'll work around it." They welcomed me back with an incredibly comfortable desk chair that I still use, and they were beyond gracious in how they worked around my limitations. When I first started back, I could only sit for about fifteen minutes at a time and then I'd have to go lay down on the couch. In those early days, a whole lot of staff meetings were held around that couch.

I enjoyed getting back into the rhythm of the world even more than I had thought I would. It was nice to have a schedule and a set routine. As the work routine began to gel again, however, the home routine was still up in the air. It's often said that we give the best of ourselves to our jobs, and our families get whatever's left. Unfortunately for my family, there really wasn't much left by the time I got home. My feet and back hurt so bad sometimes that I'd be sobbing on the drive home. On those days, the pain meds wouldn't cut it and I'd bring that all home, cloaked in a really bad mood, and all four of us would suffer through it.

As the weeks wore on, the doctors had some good news and some not so good news, but I was mostly in a holding pattern of general maintenance and waiting to see if the nerves in my legs and feet would reroute themselves. It would take more than a year to know. Until then there was little to do but wait. My least favorite thing.

Eventually the back brace came off for good and I wasted no tears saying goodbye. I was still on crutches as the new year began, and by then I could do more than just crutch around the house, I could crutch around the whole block. Generally, I'd say I was "okay." I might even have said I was doing "good," but unfortunately I got a look at a picture of myself that was taken right around Christmas. I looked as pale as a ghost, really thin, and just not healthy looking at all. I remember thinking, *This is what they mean when they say, "He looks like he fell off a cliff.*" The steady climb continued into the New Year and through the spring. Group released the *After the Fall* DVD in May, just in time for a series of summer work camps throughout the country. Thom and Group have been doing these work camps for thirty years; they're sort of like Habitat for Humanity projects for youth groups. Group locates impoverished areas all around the country where help is needed for building projects, and then brings in squads of youth groups to do the work, all at no charge to the community. It's spiritually based, but not in a way that leaves the kids rolling their eyes or thinking, "This is pointless." On the contrary, I've been amazed to see how powerful these camps are at cluing young people in to the real needs out there and connecting them with the concept of service in ways that can have a profound and lifelong effect. It's a phenomenal program.

It was into this phenomenal program that Thom thrust me one week in May.

Each camp lasts for five days, and each night there's a devotion session based on a theme. That year, the plan was for *After the Fall* to be a regular feature of the program.

I was with Thom in the back of the crowd at one of the very first camps when he asked me to get up and speak. Hundreds of eyes focused on me as I tried not to hyperventilate. It was a classic chirping-cricket moment as I tried to come up with something—anything—to say.

I am not just being my own worst critic when I say that my speech, when I finally did speak, was absolutely terrible. It's almost impossible to capture in words. Imagine something along the lines of, "So, what I did wrong was, like, I fell off a cliff . . . but God was really cool . . . and then, you know, I came home . . ."

I was so unprepared. Given how much of my life today involves public speaking, you'd have thought that during that first speech the clouds parted and a ray of light shined down upon me, but nothing could be further from the oratory homicide I committed that night. All I wanted to do was get off the stage, and I rushed through the story almost as fast as I could.

Thom caught up with me later as I was slinking out of the auditorium. What I've always liked about my relationship with Thom is that we can both be very open and frank. He was encouraging and told me what I had done well, but I could tell just by the way he'd "started with the positive" that something important was coming. As he spoke, he mentored me in a way I'll never forget. *He* was the ray of light.

"You can never shortchange what happened to you," he told me. "You have to tell people just like you're telling it for the first time, *every* time. It doesn't matter if you've told it a thousand times over; most people don't know your whole story. They may have heard pieces, but the only way they're going to see and understand how powerful God is, and what He really did for you, is to hear it all. Otherwise you lose the impact of what happened, and then lose the impact of your whole story. You can never forget what a big thing God has done with you."

To me, it was as if God was trying to say, "Hey dummy, if you're going to do this, you need to do it right."

I took the advice to heart. I went home and over the next several days worked up a strong outline of how I would tell my story from then on. Just having that ready gave me confidence and even got me a little more interested in speaking again.

Initially, there was talk of me going to all ninety work camps over the summer in order to take photos of the camp activities and document what was happening, but that plan was short-lived. Because of the *After the Fall* video, it actually became impossible to work during the camps because I'd get absolutely mobbed by the kids. Sooner or later the call would ring out, "Hey! You're the guy in the video!" and for the rest of the day any attempt at work was hopeless.

After a couple experiences like that it became pretty clear that sending me to shoot photos at the camps wasn't going to work. That was okay with me because physically I just couldn't do it anyway. Pain and fatigue would put me down for the count after only a few hours. It was better to keep me home.

I didn't get another chance to test-drive my new speech at work camps that year. But that was okay; the more I thought about it, the more I realized I didn't want to be some star attraction at the camps. That just wasn't me; nor in my mind was it a good fit for the spirit and purpose of the program. Outside the camp structure, though, I could see the faintest glimmer that I could do this speaking thing more. Maybe not a lot more, but every now and then.

Before I knew it, July 21 came around again. It had been exactly one year since the accident. Everyone around me made note of it in a similar way. Cyndy looked back and marveled at how much our family had been through. Co-workers and friends said the fact that I could look ahead to the future and be excited about it, knowing that I should have been dead or paralyzed, was a marvel in itself. Some even told me that July 21 was my new birthday.

While everyone else was thankful, I couldn't help feeling that I'd just lost a whole year of my life. At least I could believe that the worst was over. Though I was wrong about that.

I'd never thought of it that way. For me, the anniversary was not as big a deal, and I observed it much differently than everyone else. If anything, while others were marveling at how far I'd come in a year, I was thinking about how fast a year had gone by and how far I still had to go. I was still in a cast, still struggling with my leg, and still unable to stand for long periods of time. While everyone else was thankful, I couldn't help feeling that I'd just lost a whole year of my life. At least I could believe that the worst was over. Though I was wrong about that.

One day in fall, I started having girl-screaming-in-a-horror-movie pain in my right foot and ankle. It wasn't some dull ache that just welled up; it was an instant, ramming pain that was worse than anything I had experienced throughout the entire ordeal of my fall and recovery. Like someone was breaking my leg with a bat over and over again. If anyone even touched the skin I'd start howling. The pain would sneak up and hit me out of nowhere and it was so bad it made me puke. If you want a sense of what it was like, have someone grab a pair of pliers and pinch the skin between your thumb and forefinger as hard as they can for five minutes. Then imagine that pain in your whole lower leg.

And it kept getting worse. It'd last for an hour sometimes, then break, and come back again, instantly at full strength. I didn't understand what was happening, and I didn't want anyone to see me like that when it started. I'd just go off by myself somewhere and hiss and spit through it. It took only one day to realize that I couldn't just endure it. I couldn't even sleep. There was no escape from it unless it decided on its own to go away.

I called Doug Lundy, my orthopedist, told him what was going on, and asked if he knew what was happening. He told me it was one of two things.

"You've either got an infection, or if not that, then I think I know what it is," he said. "If it's infected though, that leg is coming off."

"That's fine. I don't care," I said. After all my abhorrence of amputation, and insistence that it wasn't going to happen, I was ready to cut the thing off myself. It hurt that bad.

He didn't bother to tell me at the time what he thought the other possibility might be. He just told me to come in and get some blood drawn. We went to his office that very day. I was beyond a wreck. The poor girl who got the job of drawing my blood got the brunt of it. Before she even touched me, I warned her, "If you hurt me, I'm going to hurt you." Not exactly the love of Jesus.

Dr. Lundy said they were going to rush the tests through but I'd still have to wait until the next morning for the results.

Cyndy and I drove home and I started what would be the longest night of my life. I kept thinking how insane this had become. I was supposed to be getting better. I was supposed to be getting back to my old life, or most of it anyway. Between the pain and the near panic, I spent another night completely without sleep.

When the phone rang the next morning I was ready for news that my life was about to change in a way I had never before considered in my wildest dreams.

Lundy cut right to the chase. There was no infection.

"Your blood's clean," he said, "which means I have a pretty good idea what's going on. I have a colleague, Dr. MacGregor.* He's a neurosurgeon. You need to go see him. They have your file already."

The best way to describe my state at that point is punch-drunk. I was going on forty-eight hours of no sleep, pain had been wracking my body almost the whole time, and I'd just been through the most emotionally trying twenty-four hours of my life. I was not processing anything. No infection was good news, right? Okay, then what was wrong with me? I just thanked him, hung up, and called MacGregor's office.

---

* Not his real name.

They'd been expecting to hear from me and had an appointment available that morning. In a few hours I was sitting on an exam table talking to the man himself.

Dr. MacGregor was a tall man with a birdlike face. He had piercing but squinty eyes and a sharp nose that gave his face an intense look that was a bit unnerving. He's clearly a brilliant brain surgeon, but that gift came at a cost. At best, he had a passionless, Dr. Spock-like personality . . . and that's being kind.

I explained my pain to him, what it felt like, the frequency, the duration, everything I could think of. When I was done, he nodded once. Then he touched my leg lightly and sent me right through the ceiling.

"I'll be right back," he said. It was not the apology I expected.

He left the room and came back a few seconds later with a handful of medical brochures that he thrust toward me as he spoke.

"You have Reflex Sympathetic Dystrophy, and you'll probably be confined to a wheelchair in about six months. My aide will be right in."

With that, he left the room.

If I'd had more sleep and presence of mind I probably would have screamed after him as he was leaving. Something along the lines of *"Are you freaking kidding me?!"* might have captured the sentiment, but it would have come out in language much more suited to burly navy men in dockside bars. Instead, I was speechless. I'd just taken another one right on the chin. The room felt hot and my leg, for once, didn't hurt. Or if it did, I didn't care at that moment. I don't know why I didn't pass out.

The aide was in the room in less than two minutes. Whatever the avian Dr. MacGregor lacked in compassion, he more than made up for in smarts, starting with his decision to hire people who knew his limitations and could talk his patients back in off the ledge.

The aide told me she was there to help and explained it all to me. "You have a gate in your brain that opens to pain when you get hurt, and sometimes it opens up and we can't shut it," she said. "The good news is we know what it is. The bad news is it's an incurable disease. We can manage it, but we just don't know yet how to make it go away."

The disease comes from heavy trauma to a nerve, which I'd done in the fall. The nerve gets damaged so badly that when it's repaired it only remembers the last thing it felt. In my case, that was lots and lots of pain, and so that's all it gave me.

I looked at the literature as the aide stepped out for a moment to get me some drug samples and a prescription. I saw no love in what I was reading. It was all about wheelchairs, surgically implanted pain pumps, and making the victim comfortable until they die. The pain was likely to get worse over time and spread up my leg and to other parts of my body. Amputation might help, but it might not. It might even make things worse.

If there was any good news, it was that I'd been diagnosed early, but that only meant treatment could start sooner.

It was like being given a death sentence, in which my body would die a slow, exceedingly painful death while I was trapped inside.

The aide came back with a sample pack of drugs and a prescription for more. They were putting me on something called Neurontin, which is actually a seizure drug. She told me it would help with the pain and the problem. Essentially, it pushes the gate closed for some undetermined amount of time. She also explained that I'd be taking it for the rest of my life. Some days I might only need half a pill. Other days I might need to cram down five at a time.

"When the pain hits you hard, you have to hit back, just as hard," she said.

I sprinted right into full denial. I was sure they were both wrong. I was sure there were no wheelchairs in my future, and no way was I amputating my leg to stop this.

I took three of the pills on my way out the door and walked back to my truck. The pain in my leg was so intense I had to wait to drive. Then twenty minutes later, as I was making my way home, a switch turned off and my leg stopped hurting. That's when I knew MacGregor and his aide were right. I had RSD.

What really pissed me off was that no one had told me about this. I'd never even heard of RSD before. I learned it was rare, but if there had only been some kind of heads-up that something like this could happen I might have been a little more prepared.

Cyndy could tell from the instant I walked in the door that the appointment had not gone well. I still had all the literature from MacGregor's office with me. I just walked over and handed everything to her.

"This is what I have," I said, my voice conveying even less emotion than MacGregor had. I didn't wait for a response. I just went to the bedroom to lie down.

I had some choice words for God, starting with something much stronger than "what the heck?" I had been as faithful as I could since the accident and had healed well. Now all of a sudden I was facing amputation and wheelchairs. I wondered just what would have happened if I *hadn't* been so obedient and faithful through it all. Everything was completely screwed up.

Where did this come from? I asked finally. *Here we were, everything was going along just fine. We had hope, we had plans, we were starting to think our lives would be predictable and safe, and now You've pulled the rug out from under me again. This isn't healing me—this is going backward. This is insane. Thanks so much for the letdown.*

In the other room, Cyndy was looking at the brochures and reaching the end of her own rope. All of a sudden her husband, who had been steadily returning to normal, was completely screwed. She slipped into depression and cried out to God. After all the countless hours of stress, of holding it together, of sheer gutting it out, she finally hit her limit, gave up, and said, "Enough!"

What she gave up was trying to control our situation. She didn't want to keep trying to hold all the pieces of our family and life together, build it up to something stable, and then see it all get knocked down again like a stack of toy blocks. Instead she did what we both should have done from the start. She gave everything over to God. She realized this was so screwed up, there was no way either of us—together or alone—could come close to fixing it ourselves.

As the initial shock wore off, Cyndy and I started to talk about it. We looked at all the brochures and papers together, more closely than I had in MacGregor's office, to try to get a grip on the situation. It's a lot easier to focus when you don't want to punch somebody in the face.

A deeper dive into the papers, however, offered no reassurance. The RSD was going to travel up my leg, into my hips, and over to the other side of my body in what seemed like an inevitable and relentless march that would be so debilitating that it'd leave me in a wheelchair with no hope of ever getting out.

We went online next, and that was a huge mistake. Everything MacGregor and these papers had to say was brought to life in vivid color with pictures and testimonials. Before long we just shut the computer off, unable to take any more. We went to bed all but certain I'd be living in a wheelchair in a matter of months. There was not even a spark of "I'm going to fight this" in me. There was no thinking ahead or planning. It was a complete shutdown.

I was no less depressed the next morning, but I was a little more pragmatic.

I had thought I'd found a way to keep working despite my limitations, but now more limitations were about to be piled on and I had to think about what this was going to mean for my job.

I had no ideas at all, of course, just a keener sense of the problem. If I was going to be stuck in a wheelchair, my bosses needed to know about it. I didn't beat around the bush. I went into Thom's office and just tossed some of the brochures on his desk.

"This is what's wrong with me," I said. "I have no idea what to do, but I'll be at home trying to figure this out."

I turned around and left. I knew Thom would have to process all of this too, so there was no point in trying to have a prolonged conversation. As it turned out, he was heading for the airport anyway, so it'd be a few days before we'd even see each other again. I later learned that Thom had a pretty direct conversation with HR: "I don't care what it costs or what precedent it sets, you need to do whatever needs to happen so Craig can still work. I don't care if you have to hang his desk from the ceiling."

Humbled as I was when I did finally hear about it, I shouldn't have been surprised. Thom has always been a man to walk the talk. He always knew that his work was much more than his business, and he was committed to making sure I could still earn a living for my family, regardless of the impact it had on him.

Not knowing he'd done that, however, I spent the rest of that day processing, praying, lost, angry, and depressed—not necessarily in that order. Cyndy and I tried to hold on to each other as best we could. At times like this I appreciated her strength and honesty. We decided not to tell the kids anything. They were too young to really understand anyway.

We did tell her mom though, and she generously offered to open

her home in Pennsylvania to us so I could live there in pain, not have
to work, and be close to family. I appreciated her giving nature and
caring heart, but I wasn't ready to check out like that just yet.

As more hours and prayer got wedged between me and Mac-
Gregor's diagnosis, I started to work my way out of shutdown mode,
and began to look at what was happening in the same way I looked at
every other challenge—I'd just have to figure out how to get around it.

I'd learned that approach through climbing. Anyone who's done
some climbing knows that being successful relies on working with the
weaknesses in the rock. Cracks, holes, fissures, dents . . . You have to
figure out how to use those weaknesses to your advantage to get past
difficult spots. At the time, it was lost on me that God takes the same
approach to each and every one of us, but it's something I've come to
see with incredible clarity since.

The RSD could put me in a chair, but MacGregor's aide had said if
I started to exercise a lot, and constantly stimulate the nerve, it would
make it harder for the disease to progress. It's basically a bandwidth
issue—if there's nothing else going on in the nerve, the disease can
shoot pain through me and continue its steady march. But giving the
nerve something else to think about through movement, hot and cold
wraps, and other stimulation would overload it and the disease would
have to take a backseat.

MacGregor had said I was in something of an "uncontrollable
situation," not knowing that those words were exactly what would
eventually motivate me to prove him wrong. If I could get the pain
to a level where I could function, and get around the problem, that
would be good for me. I launched into a campaign of movement and
a commitment to keep that nerve firing.

It was much harder than I thought.

I went at it for two solid months, but it never stopped the RSD
from flaring up unpredictably. The pain would come in hot electric waves that would start in my ankle and pound their way up to
my knee, without any rhyme or reason. Some days it would dictate
whether or not I went to work. I did my best to manage things with
drugs and movement, but all too soon it was clear that my victories in
this fight were only going to be small ones.

As that truth was dawning on me, the idea of amputating my leg
gained a foothold.

The doctors had all been very careful not to give me any false hopes, especially MacGregor, who I saw several times over those first weeks after the diagnosis. Amputation is by no means a cure for RSD, they said. They made it clear that it might not affect the disease at all, and there was a chance it would go higher in my leg and continue to spread.

> **As that truth was dawning on me, the idea of amputating my leg gained a foothold.**

All the same, there was also a chance that amputation could help. They left the choice to me.

I was still solidly opposed to the idea, but for the first time offered it up to God to help lead me to a decision. This became a time of constant prayer for me, of really learning how to trust in Him. I only asked Him to help me get clarity—I wasn't looking for any guarantees. I wasn't going into this with any agenda—I just wanted to learn as much as I could. And God suddenly surrounded me with people who could tell me what I needed to hear, not just what I wanted to hear. It wasn't that one person persuaded me completely one way or the other. It was a slow progression that happened one day at a time.

I started meeting more men who'd had amputations, and all of them were still very active. I, on the other hand, despite my "movement campaign," was not active, not in the ways they were and that I wanted to be again. I couldn't even play with my own kids, much less put on a climbing shoe or a ski boot and do the things that had made me who I was.

The other cold reality was that now, sixteen months after the accident, the doctors were telling me I had finally hit that intangible summit. I was as healed as I was going to get. I could decide that was that, or I could think more about taking my leg off and seeing what would happen.

The first call I made was to Malcolm, the man who had come to my house in the first few days after I'd returned home and had so horrified me by showing me his stump.

I was a little surprised when he told me he'd been expecting my call.

When we met I machine-gunned him with every question I could think of. How do you get up to pee at night? Can the leg get wet? How do you change your shoe? It was really rudimentary stuff, because that was the only frame of reference I had to work with. I didn't know enough to ask about infections, complications, or any of the more technical stuff.

Malcolm was patient, and probably more than a little amused. He answered all my questions and gave me a lot to think about.

I next talked with another guy who'd lost a leg in a boating accident. He made it very clear that the first six to twelve months after the surgery were going to be hell. "Just understand that it's going to be bad, but you will adjust," was what he kept saying.

And the chain went on as I continued to talk to guys who, like me, had been active before their accidents and were now active again.

I wanted to learn more, so I talked to the people who manufactured prosthetic limbs and got their opinions on what I might be able to do in the future. I probably talked to half a dozen people all over the country, and then I met Joe Johnson with Quorum Orthopedics.

He was in Windsor, Colorado, not too far from me, and more than one person had told me that if I was really thinking about doing this, I needed to talk to Joe.

Where everyone else simply told me what I might expect as a status quo, Joe was the first person who asked me what kind of lifestyle I wanted to live.

> My baseline goal was simply to be able to enjoy walking, playing with my kids, and leading a normal family life. But I told Joe what my real dreams were: I wanted to ride again, and maybe ski or climb.

My baseline goal was simply to be able to enjoy walking, playing with my kids, and leading a normal family life. But I told Joe what my real dreams were: I wanted to ride again, and maybe ski or climb.

Joe, an amputee himself, never blinked. He just said, "Okay. We can do that."

The thing that gave our meeting even more meaning was I found out Joe is also a believer. He told me straight up that I should pray about this, for clarity and strength. He repeated what I'd heard from others—it would be hard for the first several months, but he said someone my age and with my physical makeup should do pretty well. Then he asked me when my surgery was.

I told him I hadn't scheduled it, and that I was still making up my mind. Joe understood and just gave me a phone number for a guy he thought I should talk to. His name was Rik Heid. He was in his fifties, a member of the U.S. Paralympic Skiing team with five gold medals to his name, and a lower leg amputee.

"I want you to meet him," Joe told me. "You need to meet someone who's older, still active, having fun, and has the same kind of amputation you would."

I hadn't heard of Rik before, but I agreed to meet him right away, so Joe went about setting it up. I learned more about Rik in the intervening weeks. He'd always been a phenomenal skier, but as an amputee he was using a monoski and absolutely shredding the mountains wherever he went.

When the day finally came, I was excited about meeting him, as was Cyndy. The four of us—Rik, Joe, Cyndy, and I—met around Joe's conference table and just started bantering. Joe and Rik were telling me how much they understood that what I was thinking of doing was almost alien, but it was going to be awesome on the other side of it.

Joe and Rik are both pretty intense, and I don't think I could have found two stronger advocates for going through with it. I wasn't fully convinced yet, but I was starting to think that I could do this. I could cut my leg off, and it would be okay. I would be okay. I could reclaim my old life, or most of it, and my kids would grow up knowing me as who I really was.

The conversation got so lively that Cyndy, with a slight twinkle, jabbed, "Wow, you guys are getting pretty jazzed about cutting your leg off."

We all chuckled, but she was right. I'd reached a new high-water mark in not just being open to the idea, but starting to believe I might be better off without my leg than with it. It was much more than just being jazzed. I was starting to have hope for a better, or at least a more familiar, quality of life.

Joe and Rik also made sure I knew what the downsides were. Again I heard that even in the best-case scenario, the first few months after the operation were going to be pure hell, and only after that hurdle was cleared would it become a downhill cruise. Along the way there might be risks of infection, there might be nerve disorders, such as something called nueroma, where the nerve is too close to the skin and is a constant source of pain. Skin grafts might not heal correctly.

Dr. MacGregor had been extremely careful to tell me amputation might be able to "get above the RSD," or it could actually make it worse. There were no guarantees.

I knew from talking with Dr. Lundy that less than half of all amputees are what could be called "active," precisely because of all the potential downsides.

"That's not going to be you," he'd told me next, "but this is a big deal. You have to be 110 percent positive this is what you want to do. Because there's no going back."

Cyndy and I talked about it more on the way home from Joe's office, and we began talking about it a lot more in the following weeks. She was very good at listening, letting me ramble on and sort it out myself, but never pushing me in one direction or another. Her outward position was that this was not her leg—this was a deeply personal decision and one I needed to be comfortable with. I needed to be the one to make a decision, and she would respect it and support me no matter what it was, and no matter what happened after.

In the end, there was no dazzling epiphany. Weighing all the pros and cons led to one very simple fact: none of the potential outcomes that might result from cutting my leg off were any worse than not cutting it off and simply living with RSD. And at least with amputation, it was my own choice. I could set the rules for a change instead of reacting to the rules and the bad news that had been controlling me for the past year.

When I tell that to some people, they ask me if that was simply me not letting God be in control. It's a fair question, but I think by submitting, you have to be open to what God is going to do in your life, because He's going to be present in it in different ways. You have to be open to the cues and the road signs and pointers that are given to you. In my case it was me saying to God, "Okay, I give up trying to do whatever I can to keep my leg and trying to tell You what my healing should be." God put many people in my path, and while no single one of them filled in all the gaps, each one gave me bits and pieces that continually steered me further down the path to a decision. That decision now seemed pretty clear.

I told Cyndy where my head was and asked her what she thought. She reacted with her characteristic direct approach.

"I think you're making the right decision," she said.

That was all I needed. Although a few days later, in early November when I was back in Dr. Lundy's office, I was terrified.

It's one thing to make a decision like that in your head, but to utter it and set in motion a course of events that end with a significant piece of your body being gone is off the chart.

I gathered my thoughts and emotions, and there in his office I said the words I never thought I could.

"I want to cut my leg off."

He smiled and waited for me to go on.

"I've talked to a lot of people. I've been thinking a lot about it, and I want to take it off."

The words came out flat and hollow in the office. The voice sounded far, far away, even though I knew it was mine. I referred to my leg as "it" on purpose. It was a way of coping, a way of making it less a part of me.

Scared as I was, it was also kind of a relief. I'd finally gotten past the decision. Now I could start to move forward, as long as my doctor agreed with it.

Dr. Lundy stood right up, leaned all the way across his enormous desk, grabbed both of my shoulders and grinned at me.

"You're doing the right thing," he told me. "Don't doubt it. Grab it. Own it. Your foot is being held together with eleven pins and a plate. I knew you'd have to give it up, but it was just a matter of you getting to a place where you were ready to do it."

With that he immediately walked me right out of his office and to his scheduler, who made a surgery appointment for December 2.

"That's the day we operate," he said, tapping the calendar with his finger. "That's the day we operate and start again."

I was kind of stunned at how fast things were moving already, and started to stammer about maybe scheduling something later, but he continued to encourage me.

"You've made your decision. The longer you wait the more it's going to wear on you," he said. "Let's write a date down."

As he spoke he validated everything I'd been thinking. He'd been with me since the beginning and had a vested interest in me, and he was telling me I was on the right path. He removed the last doubts I had. At least for a few minutes.

As I walked out of his office I couldn't help feeling like that was the last time I would ever leave his office as a whole person.

"You're going to want about eight inches of stump."

There was no need for Joe to be delicate. He was in full work mode and knew exactly what he was talking about.

"You'll have about eight inches of good bone to work with, and we want as much leg as we can get," he continued. "The longer the stump, the longer the lever arm you'll have on the joint, and that's all for the better. But if you keep it too long, then you won't be able to get certain types of feet."

I had to marvel at how easily he discussed concepts that were still alien to me, but I understood what he was saying just the same.

"There's a type of foot called the Ceterus. I think it will be very responsive for you. It's the first foot I wore, but you need a stump only eight inches, otherwise you won't be able to use that foot."

He'd been studying my x-rays as we talked, making more eye contact with them than with me, until he got to his next question.

"Have you talked to your doctor about an Ertl bridge?"

My blank stare was all the response he needed, and he gave me a quick crash course. There are two bones in the lower leg, the tibia and the fibula. They are long, narrow bones that run parallel to each other. In a traditional "guillotine amputation," for lack of a better term, the ends of the bones that remain in your leg are just sort of "free floating" in the muscle. You can literally squeeze your leg and move the bones together, something the doctors like to call "chopsticking."

When you wear a prosthesis, you slide your stump into a socket that's curved at the bottom, and the nature of that design can cause your bones to chopstick in the socket. That does a job on the nerves in there and can cause a good amount of pain. It's also a lot less stable than when the bones are whole. The way God made them, they are structured perfectly to bear weight and provide support, but when the bones are cut, that structure is lost.

Without that structure in place, things like skiing, biking, and climbing would be all but impossible—my leg wouldn't be able to hold up to the pounding and stress.

An Ertl bonebridge was the solution. It was developed in Hungary in the 1920s by Dr. Janos Ertl. He discovered that, over time, the cut ends of the tibia and fibula tended to grow toward each other. He thought that if he could actually encourage this process, and facilitate bone growth between the ends of the tibia and fibula, effectively reconnecting them, he could re-create the more stable support system.

All it took was a small piece of bone from the part of the leg that was usually thrown away. That piece was grafted in between the cut ends of the leg bones, creating a bridge, and everything was left to knit together naturally.

Medically speaking, there's much more to it than that, of course, and the procedure itself has evolved a lot in the past ninety years, but Dr. Ertl's original idea was sound, and has been practiced by his sons and grandsons ever since.

What really sold me on it, though, was a video Joe showed me with two guys, one with a traditional amputation and one with an Ertl bridge. Both put their stumps on a chair and tried to balance on it. Traditional guy pretty much screamed and bailed out after a couple seconds. The Ertl guy balanced there like something out of Cirque du Soleil.

"If you're going to be the kind of person you've told me you want to be, you're going to need certain tools, and this is one of them," Joe said. "You need a certain structure in your leg, and you need to stack the deck as much as you can in your favor."

Despite how long the procedure had been around, however, it wasn't very commonly used. When I talked to Dr. Lundy about it later, he said he'd heard of it but had never done it. In fact, if that was the direction we went, and it certainly was what I wanted, I'd be the first person in Colorado to have it done. He called Dr. Jan Ertl, Janos's grandson, and talked about the procedure, and about me. Jan's opinion was not hard to interpret.

"He's a perfect candidate."

When Dr. Lundy and I talked about it again, he was on board. It would require a longer healing process, ten weeks instead of the usual eight, but he thought it made sense for me and wanted to give it a go.

That whole chain of events was another example of God open-ing all the right doors at the perfect time for me. I was literally a few weeks from my amputation when Joe told me about the Ertl bridge. If I hadn't ever found Joe, or if I'd gone with someone else, who knows, I might never have known about the procedure and might be living a very different life today. Instead, I was able to work more with Joe, now that we knew what my leg was going to be after the surgery, and we had a foot and socket designed before I even went to the hospital. It was a little weird, seeing what I'd be walking on. That was assuming there were no infections or complications of course, but going into the surgery you really can't obsess over those things. You have to commit yourself to best-case-scenario thinking, and seeing the foot design made that easier. It took a lot of the mystery out of the future and, with that, some of the fear of the unknown, but certainly not all.

> **My prayer life over those several weeks was more like an ongoing dialogue with God; my very thoughts were inter-twined with prayer.**

I had been praying my brains out ever since I'd made the appointment in Dr. Lun-dy's office, to the point that my prayer life over those several weeks was more like an ongoing dialogue with God; my very thoughts were intertwined with prayer. There were only a few weeks to go before my surgery, but that was plenty of time for doubts to creep in and for me to second-guess myself over and over again. The finality of it all began to weigh on me. My leg below the knee was going to be gone. Forever. What if it really wasn't the right thing to do? It got pretty stressful.

I asked God to show me beyond the shadow of a doubt that I was doing the right thing. And there would be little signs here and there. One day on a drive to Fort Collins I saw a guy with only one leg on a bike, and he was just cranking up this hill. It was another reassurance that everything really was going to be just fine. I'd be thankful for those moments, but none of them were enough to push me firmly into Camp Confidence. I was like Gideon, continually asking God for just one more sign.

In *The North Face of God*, Ken Gire writes, "In our own experi-ence with God, at some time or another, we have all encountered the silence of Heaven." As I trudged toward the date of cutting off my leg, I struggled and argued with God, asking Him why this needed to happen and why I had to go through this test.

To add to the confusion, my foot actually began feeling better. My ankle was feeling the best it had in eighteen months, and I had to wonder if there was more healing ahead. After all, I had just crawled out of a big pit of pain. Did I really want to jump right back in? Maybe I was moving too fast after all.

But then again, I still couldn't do anything I wanted. The doctors had all told me that if I even tried climbing or skiing on that foot it'd shatter. Over and over again I kept coming back to my original decision: I was better off without the leg than with it.

Cyndy and I had decided to let our church community, as well as the folks at Group and other friends, know about my decision. In general people were incredibly supportive, but at the same time, I noticed that people tend to get a little weird around you when they know you're about to cut part of yourself off. There's not exactly a Hallmark card for that one. It's hard for anyone to know what to say—"Good job!" or "Are you crazy?" aren't really appropriate. Whenever we told someone it was almost like they were at a funeral, trying to be genuine and caring, but without the first clue what to do or say.

Interestingly enough, around this time I got my first formal invitation to speak. A friend of mine was a pastor at a local church that was launching its fall series with a huge men's breakfast. About three hundred guys would be there. He wanted me to come and talk about what I saw God doing in my life.

The more I thought about it, even as I agonized over my decision, I realized that I was being given a chance to show people that even though something really wicked was coming, I still believed in this God of mine and His plan for me. True, I didn't always feel that way, but I felt it enough to know that was the image I wanted to project.

I realize that might sound a little disingenuous. It wasn't that I wanted to get up in front of people and babble some feel-good platitudes that I didn't believe. In fact I had absolutely no doubt that God

> I was being given a chance to show people that even though something really wicked was coming, I still believed in this God of mine and His plan for me.

had a plan for me, I just hadn't really figured out what that plan might be yet. And at the same time, I was staring down the barrel of this coming surgery, after which any number of things could go seriously wrong, including the possibility that I could get a horrible infection and die. I just didn't want my own fears about what could happen and how bad things could get to distract people from all the amazing things God had done and was doing in my life.

I accepted the invitation and, remembering Thom's words, I gave a talk that was still somewhat rudimentary but markedly better than the first one. Of course, that's not really saying much. I took questions at the end and told them about having to go to the hospital in a couple weeks to have the amputation.

When it was over, as I was making my way toward the door, a group of about twelve men came up to me and as I made eye contact with the man in front, he spoke.

"I and the guys behind me would really like to lay hands on you," he said. "We believe God can heal your leg."

I have to confess, my first reaction to this was that my hackles got raised, and my first thought was to tell this guy he was crazy. I asked what he was talking about and he told me that if they could lay hands on me, and my faith was strong enough, God could heal my leg. It wasn't that I didn't believe God could heal my leg, but what I suddenly and very powerfully realized was that God didn't need to heal my leg.

I was about to argue the point, but for some reason I just stopped myself and said okay. I knew what "laying on of hands" was, but I wasn't a big practitioner of touching a person as I prayed for them or believing that by doing so they could be healed as Jesus had healed others. I didn't think these guys would have much luck, but it couldn't hurt. As they gathered around me, I must admit, it was a notch or two above ordinary everyday weirdness.

Then as they prayed, I had another powerful thought. I *had* been healed. God had done as I asked.

I don't remember what that small group of guys said as they prayed, but when they were done the one who'd spoken first asked me how I felt. I thanked him for what he and the others had done, and then I asked them to let me lay out for all of them what God had already done for me.

The words that came out of my mouth amounted to something I

had never articulated before, much less processed in my head. It was the very first time that God helped me see a clear glimpse of what He had in mind.

"First, you have to understand where I've come from," I said. "I went through this whole accident and endured all those things I told you had happened to my body, all those things which should have killed me or paralyzed me, but God in His wisdom said no. His plan was different.

"I really do think God could heal this leg, absolutely He could, but He doesn't have to, and I don't really think that's even His plan. If it were, He'd have done it already; and if He does heal my leg, then my story is done. It's a story I tell once and no one will ever know what happened to me. But if I'm wearing a prosthetic leg and foot, that's a much rarer thing. That's going to spur questions, and those questions are going to start conversations that will be all about my faith and what God has done for me. In a prosthetic leg, I can tell the story of my accident over and over again, and I can't possibly tell the story of my accident without talking about how God has worked in my life."

I stopped there, a little startled at myself, and how obvious that all suddenly seemed, even though it hadn't crossed my own mind for a year and a half.

The leader of the group just nodded, said he understood, and they all went on their way. I wasn't sure he truly understood, but he didn't challenge me. Later, I figured it was because there was nothing to challenge.

I left the church feeling more certain than ever that I was doing the right thing. And I continued to surround myself with people like Malcolm, Rik, and Joe who could keep me in that mind-set.

As the calendar changed to December my anxiety grew. I got really edgy and my temper was short. Even though I knew I was doing the right thing to get back to the life I loved, I was having a hard time getting my head around actually cutting my leg off. I knew that I was going to be right back in the pit of pain for a long time, and that I'd have to claw my way out of it. That was not something I was looking forward to. For six months to a year I'd be at my most frail, waiting for bones to knit.

On the night of December 1, the night before surgery, the phone rang. It was a woman from the church. I knew who she was, but I didn't really know her. I assumed she was calling to give me some words of encouragement, but within seconds I wished I had never picked up the phone.

She launched right into the fact that she thought I was making a huge mistake. Her husband, who was in his seventies, had lost his leg and was basically spending his life in bed, unable to get around and constantly in pain. She fired questions at me without letting me answer.

"Have you really thought this through? Are you sure you aren't making a bad decision? Don't you think you should look into finding some way to keep your leg?"

It was a nightmare. And it went on for almost ten minutes before I mustered as much social grace as I could, announced that I could not have this conversation, and hung up on her.

I was shaking, somewhere between extreme anger and blind panic. How could she have done that? She'd known the surgery was tomorrow, but she'd never spoken to me about it before. She had no reason, no right, to call me at one of the most pivotal moments in my entire life to tell me what I was doing was wrong.

I'm sure her heart was in the right place—her experience was very real and I'm sure it had been hard, and she really didn't want me to have to go through that. But that phone call taught me there are right ways and wrong ways to do things, and unsolicited advice can really backfire. I'm sure every woman who's ever been pregnant can identify with me on that one.

I decided I was never going to do that. If people asked me what I thought, I'd tell them, even if I knew they wouldn't like it, but until they asked I was going to keep my opinions to myself.

Hours later, when I'd finally calmed down again, I stood in my bathroom, cast off, staring at myself in the mirror and trying to come to grips with the fact that this was it. That leg was going away and things were going to be very different.

I took out a razor and wet my leg. I wanted to shave it so there would be no question about which leg to cut. I'd heard, or thought I'd heard, horror stories about doctors cutting the wrong limb off.

As I drew the razor up my leg, I knew the operation was the right thing to do, but I kept hearing that woman's voice in my head and thinking maybe I should wait longer. Maybe the pain would lessen over time. Why did I want to climb again anyway? I'd had a good run of it. Maybe it was time to stop now. It had almost killed me, and it had seemingly robbed Cyndy and me of the plans we'd made. Why would I want to give it another chance to finish the job?

Right after the accident, if I had woken up in the hospital and the leg was already gone, I would have been shocked, but I would have moved past it more easily. I'd have had no control over that. This was something I could control. I didn't have to do this. I'd simply decided that if I wanted to be able to do all the things I'd done before, this needed to happen.

Even with that in my head, I was second-guessing the whole plan all over again. What if I was worse off afterward? I'd seen some amputees who had done badly. And here I was about to be the first person in Colorado to have a special procedure done, by a doctor who had never done it before.

I shaved carefully, not wanting to cut myself, and unable to laugh at the irony.

My surgery was scheduled for 7:00 AM. They'd given me some special pills, basically tranquilizers, to take if I wanted to stay calm. I decided not to take any before going to bed because I wasn't going to sleep anyway. I saved them instead for the morning and the ride to the hospital.

Unfortunately, as Cyndy and I drove to the hospital in the early cold and dark, I discovered I was capable of a kind of anxiety that no tranquilizers could touch. It just grew and grew with every rotation of the wheels. Cyndy and I talked, but I have no idea about what. All I remember is trying not to think about what I was doing.

Okay, just one step at a time. Walk in. Sit down. Don't overthink this or you're going to absolutely freak out.

Internally, I was nervous, scared, petrified. But I followed my own advice as we parked at the hospital. We just walked into admitting, sat down, and did the paperwork. I felt like I was moving through a strange dream.

When the paperwork was done, they took us into the prep area where I changed into a hospital gown, instantly reminded of just how much I hated them. I silently pulled myself onto a gurney. I couldn't make eye contact with Cyndy. Good heavens, but those pills were useless.

A nurse came in after a couple minutes and asked me how I was. I would have been willing to let the stupidity of her question be lost to obscurity, but then she told me I did a bad job shaving my leg.

She got right to work re-shaving it and handed me a Sharpie marker.

"I need you to write an 'x' on your leg," she said.

"Why?"

"So we know which one you want to amputate."

I wrote a really, really big X on my leg and signed my name underneath it. It was one of the oddest things I had ever done in my life. Marking that X really nailed it home that I was going to cut my leg off. Shaving the night before had been weird, but to physically mark it took it out of the realm of ideas and I realized I was taking ownership of what was happening in a way I had never done before. By my own hand and my own signature, I was telling the doctor what to do.

Unfortunately that didn't ease my mind at all and, other than the pills I'd taken earlier—which I was now convinced were placebos—they hadn't started pumping any drugs into me yet to get me prepped for the operation. I expected the nurse to take my arm and tell me I was going to feel that telltale pinch of an IV going in, but she just left the room.

As the curtain closed behind her, and Cyndy and I were alone again, the realization that it was not too late, that I could still leave right now, cut through all the anxiety like a laser. I had walked into this hospital voluntarily. I could just get up, walk out, and there was nothing anybody could do to stop me.

It was much more than just an idle thought. A real fight-or-flight response was about to kick in and Cyndy could sense that I was reaching a breaking point. She told me everything was going to be fine, and she tried to be comforting, but the doubts kept creeping in. I was getting more and more agitated. At the very second I was about to reach my limit, I saw someone out of the corner of my eye. I turned and saw my pastor, Glen, standing there, out of breath.

I hadn't asked him to come, and seeing him standing there panting was so out of place that I asked the dumbest question I could.

"Glen? What are you doing here?"

Glen is at his core a very mellow person, to the point that even just seeing him there and knowing his personality as I did, I was immediately comforted. A little. I had never seen him out of breath before, so I was still within a few inches of the brink, but his answer was so honest and straightforward and so characteristically Glen that I was soon set almost completely at ease.

"I'm here to pray with you. Sorry I was late."

He'd only known the date and time of my surgery, and which hospital, but no other details. He'd spent the last several minutes literally running through the place looking for me, and was trying now to catch his breath.

I can't fully explain what I felt. After a morning of feeling lost and alone, there was no doubt in my mind that God had just shown up. And as always, it was in His own perfect timing, when it would have the greatest impact.

The three of us held hands and prayed right there. We prayed for comfort for me and Cyndy, for guidance and wisdom for the doctors, and for my safety. When we were done we said "Amen," the curtain opened, and Dr. Lundy was standing right there looking me full in the eyes.

"You're doing the right thing," he said.

I want to say here that despite the jokes and the TV dramas about how surgeons always want to cut into people, the fact is that there are some surgeries they'd rather not have to do. In the world of doctors, an amputation is a loss. They can't save the limb, and that's a hard thing to accept, even for the best of them. For Dr. Lundy to say that to me, that I was doing the right thing after everything he'd done to try to save my leg, meant much more than the words alone could have possibly conveyed.

It was clearly God stepping in and telling me, "Not only am I going to show you this is the right decision, and you're going to be okay, but you're going to hear it from the two men that you respect and trust most in the world."

And there was no more doubt or panic. When God had Glen and Dr. Lundy line up the way they had, to be there and assure me in quick succession, the last of my anxiety disappeared. They were able to tell me something I couldn't hear from myself or Cyndy or anyone else. It gave me the clarity I needed to say, "Okay, let's do this now."

The IV went in, and I felt the old familiar cold seeping through me as the really good drugs started kicking in. I told Cyndy I loved her, and they took me away. I floated just above the gurney as they wheeled me into the operating room, the lights on the ceiling once again looking oddly like stripes on the road as we went by. I was coherent, but I was good and stoned—and chatty with the doctors, most of whom I knew. Lundy asked me why I was still awake and I told him it was because I wanted to see the operating room. I wanted to see the equipment they were going to use. He agreed, first telling me there is a reason they called this "Black & Decker surgery."

I'd expected all the equipment to be pristine white, but the first thing he showed me was basically a Sawsall.

The look on my face must have convinced everyone that I had seen enough. I heard someone say, "Okay, it's time," and the lights went out.

The surgery took two hours, and as postoperative wake-ups go, this one was the best I ever had. I woke up feeling incredibly good.

In the recovery room, they told me right away not to be shocked when I sat up and looked at my legs.

I guess most people aren't ready to see what it looks like when one of your legs isn't there anymore, but I was fully prepared for what I'd see. In the medical world they might consider amputation a loss, but in my mind it was a release from the prison I'd been in for eighteen months. And when I finally could sit up and take a look, there was a moment of, *Wow, it's really gone . . .* and then it was right on to, *Okay, that's done. I'm glad that's behind me. I'm ready to move on.*

Dr. Lundy came in the room after a few minutes and asked me how I was doing. I told him I felt great.

"I don't even hurt at all," I told him. "I think I could go home. I'm ready to crutch out of here right now."

I wasn't kidding either. I really felt good. Of course, the anesthesia hadn't worn off yet.

He was glad to hear I felt so good, but he made it pretty clear they were going to keep me overnight.

Cyndy was in the room with me and, as Dr. Lundy ducked out to do whatever it is doctors have to do sometimes, we had a nice little reunion. I told her I was doing really well, and everything she read in my eyes and on my face was proof I was telling the truth.

"I'll be home tomorrow," I told her. "It's okay if you want to go home and be with the kids, and tell them I'm okay. I'm good here."

She stayed a little longer, but being convinced all really was well, she went home.

And I was great until 11:00 that night, when the epidural finally wore off. My pain level rocketed up from 0 to 13 in half an hour, and I made sure everyone knew it.

Unfortunately, nothing they were doing was working. I was taking morphine by the bagful, but I'd built up such a tolerance to painkillers over the past year and a half that it just wasn't having any effect. By the third bag they told me they couldn't give me any more or it'd kill me. They realized they needed to call Dr. Lundy, because something was very wrong. It was three in the morning and between the pain and the volume of morphine in me I was puking my guts out.

They finally got Lundy on the phone at 4:30 and he was furious.

The staff had been told I'd been taking Tramadol which, to cut to the chase, meant morphine wasn't going to work. They should have known that.

I was in so much pain by that point that the only thing he could do was order another spinal, which he did.

No human anesthesiologist could have possibly gotten to me fast enough to put me in a pleasant mood, but when the one who finally showed up tried to take a few extra seconds and tell me about the risks, I cut him off and told him how things were going to go.

"I don't care if I'm paralyzed," I hissed. "Just shut up and do it."

I didn't even feel the prick. All I knew was that the pain was gone instantly. I wanted to cry.

Dr. Lundy arrived at the hospital about a half hour later and made sure the staff understood the step-down plan for getting me off the pain meds that he wanted implemented. When he was done with them he came to me and told me how sorry he was. It wasn't supposed to have gone like that. I was in no mood to hold a grudge with anybody anymore.

I ended up in the hospital for four days while they weaned me off the hard stuff. On day two, they brought my crutches over and wanted me to stand up. I complied, but I was not expecting what happened next. Two people stood on either side of me. I thought it was just to help me balance.

I'd been lying in a bed, prone, for the past twenty-four hours so when I stood up, gravity took charge and the blood rushed down into my lower body, including my legs. For a fresh amputee, that comes with a very new, unique, and piercing kind of pain.

I thought I was going to die.

It felt like all the stitches at the bottom of my stump were going to rip open and everything inside was going to come spilling out all over the floor. And they made me stand there for a full minute, until I could get it under some kind of control. The people on either side of me weren't there for balance. They were to catch me in the very likely event that I passed out.

When I sat back down I was angry again. No one had told me about that, there had been no warning. Yeah, I'd heard what they'd said about the first six months being hell, but they could have said something about *this!*

The rest of my four days in the hospital were more of that same pain parade as they stepped me down off the meds. I couldn't really eat or sleep much. It was pretty miserable. They needed me to move around as much as possible, because the more I was on my feet, so to speak, the more I'd get used to the discomfort and the less it'd hurt. Sure. Whatever.

My new prosthesis wasn't ready yet, not that I could have worn it anyway. They had me in something called a rigid dressing—it looks kind of like a knee brace and, true to its appearance, it locks your leg so you can't bend your knee at all. That was important so my hamstrings wouldn't shrink. At the same time it protected the end of my leg so it could heal.

On day four my mother-in-law came into town and the hospital staff asked me if I wanted to go home. I'd earned a doctorate in hating the hospital by then, so I was all for it. They wheeled me out to Cyndy and the car and I pulled myself in, little knowing what a festival of horrors a forty-minute car ride would be. The cold made my leg hurt. Every bump in the road made my leg hurt. Thinking about how much my leg hurt made my leg hurt. It was torture.

By the time we got home I was just dying, the pain was so intense.

I went right into the bedroom, bypassing Cyndy's mom without so much as a hello, and collapsed.

I was supposed to be on bed rest for the next seven weeks, not putting any serious weight on my leg and just letting it heal. But after about a week I was finally convinced that I really would get used to things, and for some reason I went back to work. I still took it easy, but I had no business being there, especially since my center of gravity had been completely thrown off and I hadn't quite recalibrated yet.

Sure enough, one day in the studio I was ambling along, got hung up on something, and pitched forward. For thirty-nine years, whenever I'd tripped, I'd stuck my foot out to catch myself. This time, there was no foot.

I landed squarely on the end of the stump and I don't know what got my heart rate going more, the white-hot electric pain that ricocheted through me, or the fear that I had just shattered all the work Dr. Lundy had done. Someone called Cyndy, who screeched over in the car and took me to the hospital. I was sure I'd broken bones, but the x-rays proved me wrong. I was lucky, but the look in everyone's eyes said the same thing: Stupid should hurt.

I went back home and did what I was told so my leg could heal right. I was still at great risk for infection, and all the bad things that could happen had the odds stacked in their favor at first. All I could do was wait it out.

I was back into the pit of pain and depression. None of the admonitions about how things would get better after six months or so did anything for me. Everything associated with that stump was pain. When I did go back to work again, this time with Dr. Lundy's blessing, I would come home so exhausted that I felt like I'd taken ten steps backward. I wasn't seeing any upside. The pain was worse than anything I thought I'd signed up for, and there was nothing I could do about it now. There was no going back.

For the first three months after the surgery, I must have second-guessed the decision twenty times a day. I got really depressed, thinking to myself that maybe if I had waited, I might have healed. I'd sort of had things under control before the operation, and now I didn't.

And then the RSD came back. It was exactly the same pain as before, but it was in a different spot, higher up my leg and occasionally getting into my hip. I remember my first thought was, *Great, now I don't have my leg, and the RSD is back. Oh-for-two.*

I went back to Dr. MacGregor right away, who spent his first words nervously reminding me that he'd warned me this could happen and that amputation was no guarantee. I told him I had no interest in suing him. I didn't care what he'd told me before. The RSD was back and I wanted it managed.

And so we set about finding the right doses of meds I'd need so I could try to work around RSD for the rest of my life. To Dr. MacGregor's credit, we found the magic number fairly soon, and things got much better very quickly.

I began to remember that I had trusted in God for this decision, and that He had all of this worked out already. I just had to be patient.

And sure enough, over time, God gave me my life back.

9

CLIMBING AGAIN

Just like we all have to learn to roll over and crawl before we can walk, I had to relearn everything about how my body worked.

Actually, re*learn* isn't quite it. I had to re*program* everything about how my body worked, starting with not being surprised every time I looked at my prosthetic leg. It's a very strange feeling to look down and see a silver and black piece of hardware attached to your body. A friend told me it was cool looking, but for me it was just alien.

With my lower right leg gone, my center of gravity had shifted. Even just standing up straight required concentration at first, but by three months after the surgery I had things fairly well dialed in. I was walking again—for a couple hours a day anyway. That was about how long I could wear my new leg for a single stretch before it got uncomfortable. I'd started out wearing it for a half hour a day and had been building up ever since.

In those early months I was also pretty terrified of everything. Even a minor injury at that stage would not be so minor. I was constantly reminding myself, and others, of how fragile I was, and had been for the past two and a half years. For the first thirty-eight years of my life I hadn't spent too much time laboring over the what-ifs, but now I had to think about them with literally every step.

Before I lost my leg, walking was just as simple and natural as breathing. Like every other human being, I just put one foot in front of the other without thinking about it. I'd make eye contact with the people around me, say hello, even chew gum. But when I walked in my prosthesis, I couldn't feel my foot hitting the ground. If you've ever tried to walk after your foot fell asleep you have kind of an idea of what that's like.

If I tried to walk "normally," it was almost inevitable that I'd pile up sooner or later. I had to learn to look at the ground as I walked so I could actually see my foot hitting the ground, scan the surrounding terrain and adjust accordingly. Even the smallest gaps in the sidewalk or uneven features on the ground would trip me up if I didn't see them first.

I learned quickly that people freak out when they see a guy with one leg trip and fall. Some would rush over to help, others would just stand in place, mouths agape, as I grunted myself back up again. It got kind of amusing, but over time that discovery was dwarfed by the realization of how amazing the human foot is because of all the things it does to keep us upright and balanced—none of which a solid prosthetic foot can do.

For just one example, all of us at one time or another have stepped off a curb when we weren't ready and, other than some slight surprise and mild embarrassment, we've come away unscathed. That's because the muscles in our feet and lower leg have flexed and stretched and adjusted to absorb the shock. On a solid prosthetic foot, there's no give whatsoever. It's like landing on a pole. You get a nice shot of pain and usually end up in a heap.

I had to learn how to go down steps again because I didn't have an ankle to bend back and forth anymore. Chances are you never thought about the fact that when you go down steps you put your toes on the front of each step and work your way down. I, however, thought about that quite a bit in those first months. This was something not even the occupational therapists could really grasp, or teach, because they had two normal feet. The technique, I discovered, was to put my heel on the front of the step, then kind of rock forward and let it fall off. It's a delicate ballet move; the trick was to find the sweet spot so I didn't catapult myself face-first into the floor, like the ED 209 in *Robocop*.

It was not something I figured out overnight. Usually I'd just be ambling along, not paying enough attention, and the next thing I knew I was in a pile on the ground asking myself what the heck had just happened. It kept me humble.

As spring faded and summer dawned I was ready to get back into an active life. How active I could be was a function of how willing I was to let my real and imagined limitations dictate what I could and could not do. The leg was clunky and very painful most of the time—even rolling on the liners that held it in place was a lesson in pain—but I learned to push through it and started taking real steps back into my old life.

Getting back on a bicycle was pretty easy. For obvious reasons, almost everyone I talked to about it told me to stay away from "clip-in" pedals, which require a special shoe that locks in to the pedal for a more efficient and powerful stroke. The problem was that when I took their advice and went riding for the first time, I was riding as if I was still using clip-ins. I had the hardest time making it up hills because my prosthetic foot kept lifting off the pedal. Then I couldn't get it back on the pedal right away, because I couldn't feel anything, so I'd have to look down for it. By then I'd lose all my momentum and just keel over like a dying buffalo.

I went home and put on the clip-in pedals, but kept the lock as loose as possible so I could twist my foot out quickly if I needed to.

After I slammed to the ground the sixth time I had an epiphany.

I'd been trying to twist my right foot, the prosthetic one, out of the lock to steady myself, because that's how I'd always done it before. My right leg had been my dominant one. The problem was, again, I had no ankle. I couldn't twist the foot out of the lock the way I needed to, even on the loosest setting. By the time I finally worked it free, I was already on the deck.

I changed tactics and tightened the cleat on my right side to its max level so my foot simply wouldn't come out unless I did an end over end. That forced me to learn to pull my left foot out of the cleat for balance. It was a learning process, but it worked.

———

Skiing, by comparison, was a little trickier.

We'd always been a family that skied together, and as winter came around I'd seen enough evidence to convince me that skiing was a "good amputee sport."

It never occurred to me to do what most of the other guys did—take off my leg and ski with outriggers. I had a prosthetic foot after all; I was going to use it. I took a drill to my ski boot and retrofitted the whole thing to accommodate my fake leg. Thinking I really had something here, I was pretty proud of myself when I stuffed the fake foot into the boot, locked it in to the ski binding and stepped into the leg. It just felt like it would work.

I headed up to the mountains with my friend George a few days later. I'd wanted to go with Cyndy at first, but after I kicked it around a little I told Cyndy for this first trip that I thought it'd be better if she stayed home so I could work out the kinks and eat a little snow without worrying her. She totally agreed.

Things went, in a word, perfectly. I felt steady and smooth getting on the lift, getting off, and skiing a couple moderate blue runs. My balance was good, the cold was refreshing, and I was cutting some nice S-curves. I felt amazingly normal—just another regular guy out on the slopes.

What I hadn't planned on was how that refreshing cold air would cause my stump to contract, ever so slightly. Nor had I considered how all the twisting and bending to make those lovely S-curves might, perchance, cause the lock on my fake leg to disengage.

Those possibilities became quite obvious though, as we were on the ski lift halfway up the mountain, and my leg fell off.

There were a lot of teenagers on the lift behind us, laughing and chattering as teenagers do. A ski lift isn't exactly a loud place, but at that moment as ski, boot, and prosthetic foot tumbled forty feet down into the snow, that lift went as quiet as death in space. I could hear the people behind me holding their collective breath.

I was stunned for a second myself, speechless. There's a kind of denial where you don't want to believe what's happened, and then there was this, where I could not believe what had just happened. It just wasn't possible.

Then I noticed that the lift chair was bouncing up and down.

I looked over at George, who was laughing so hard he was convulsing, and doing a poor job of trying to hide it. Somehow just seeing him like that got me going, and in two seconds both of us were absolutely howling, tears streaming out of our eyes, and barely able to hold on to the chair.

Of course, all that time the lift was still moving. I was going to have to dismount on one ski—a true accident waiting to happen. I remember there was a young girl working at the top of the lift who had seen it all and was busting a gut laughing as I put my one ski tip up and hoped for the best.

It was one of the hardest things I ever did, my balance was so out of whack, but I pulled it off. I came to a rest a little disappointed at the lack of applause.

"It's four chairs behind you," the girl said as I did my best to look cool. The leg had landed in a snow drift at the base of one of the lift's support towers and, fortunately, had neither hit anyone nor slid all the way downhill on its own.

Sure enough, a ski patrol guy came off the lift a minute later holding my leg up like a trophy.

"That's got to be the funniest thing I ever saw," he said, handing me his prize. For myself, I hadn't laughed that hard since before the accident, and it felt really good. It washed away a lot of bad stuff.

With that trip, I was confident that biking and skiing were once again a part of my lifestyle. As good as that was though, the real measure of who I was going to be in this new life would be gauged by whether or not I could climb. Or if I even wanted to.

The truth was, other than a mild curiosity and a notable inability to comprehend a life without climbing, I can't say I was eager to get back to it. I had loved climbing for seventeen years, and look what it had done to me. I felt a bit like a lover who'd been betrayed.

It wasn't that I was afraid. I just didn't know if I was willing to trust it again as such a big part of my life. There was a small part of me that knew I wanted to climb, but there was a much bigger part of me that just didn't know if I *needed* to.

It's not like my doctors were big fans of the idea either. They were categorically against it in fact. I had a back full of metal, a neck that had never healed right, and a junk left ankle. And those were my strong points. If I fell again, even just a little bit, and hit ground, bones would break but metal would stay in place. Paralysis was pretty much a foregone conclusion. One way or another, it'd all be over.

Climbing again was the elephant in the room for the better part of a year. I didn't want to bring it up to Cyndy, not knowing what she thought about it. I wondered if she would be absolutely opposed to the idea, even while I realized that was ridiculous. We both knew better than that.

When we did talk about it for the first time, she didn't push me one way or the other, even though she knew as much as I did that climbing was more than just a part of who I was. It was a part of who *we* were. Some of our first dates had been climbing trips together, and all through our marriage it had been a cornerstone of our lives.

She told me that if I never went back to it she was completely okay with that, but I know in her head she was wondering how very different a person I was going to be if I never climbed again. That wasn't good or bad, it was just another sobering dose of reality that the rest of our marriage was going to be very, very different from the one we had started together.

Cyndy of course continued to climb with friends, and even with our daughter, Mayah, who was getting to be quite the confident and capable little outdoorswoman. I came to really miss being outdoors with my family, so I started going along with them and keeping Will company while the ladies worked the rock walls. Before the accident, I couldn't even look at a rock wall without wanting to climb it. A strange excitement would come all over me—I'd see routes up and I'd just want to go for it. Anyone who's had a natural inclination for something knows exactly what I'm talking about. I expected that same old stirring to come back again when I went out with Cyndy and the kids after the fall, but it didn't. I wasn't sure what to make of that.

Left on my own to stew on it, I might never have done more than watch my family on those climbing excursions. Or, who knows, maybe one day out of sheer frustration I might have just gone for it. All I can say for certain is that God sometimes pushes us in just the way we need, and I would have never guessed that an innocent question from my daughter would thrust me into an experiment in faith and fear.

We were with friends at a place called Wild Iris in Shoshone National Park. Cyndy had just worked a small route on a 40-foot wall and Mayah, being the unstoppable force that she was, wanted to try it too. As routes go it was about as easy as you can get, a 5.8 on the Yosemite scale. In other words, any seven-year-old could do it, as Mayah adeptly proved in only a few minutes.

I belayed her as she worked her way up, and then lowered her to the ground. As she was unclipping from her harness and I was thinking to myself what a perfect July day it was, Mayah hit me in an unprotected flank.

"Are you going to climb next, Daddy?" Her voice reflected every bit of the sweet little girl she was. She caught me completely off guard.

I could have easily said no, but the way she asked me, it seemed so benign, as if she'd simply asked if I was going to have seconds on dessert.

"I just might do that," I told her, trying not to let my voice show that I was scared out of my mind.

Cyndy didn't say a word and neither did Jeff, the friend who had come along with us, until he offered to belay me. Had either of them given me an out, I might have taken it, but they only left me with one respectable path forward.

I tied in and checked my harness three times. I'd tied into a harness so many times before that it was still doable almost without a thought—just double up a figure-eight knot and you're good to go.

"Okay," I said. "Here we go."

"Okay, Dad," Mayah said back. "Bye!" Everything in her tone told me that since she'd had so much fun, I should go do the same. I think that simplicity is what got me moving. There was no need to overanalyze what was happening.

I checked my harness again, and checked Jeff's just for good measure. I remember as I put my hands on the rock it felt warm. The texture was sublime, perfect for climbing . . . coarse but not too rough.

I took a second to think about God, and the Max Lucado devotional, and how I'd learned that God is with us in all things. Then I took a deep breath, grabbed a handhold, and took a step on the rock face.

Pain shot through me right away, all through my leg and back. Not debilitating, just distracting.

Push through it, I told myself. *Climb through it.*

I was keenly aware that I had some fused vertebrae and that I hadn't done any exercises that would prepare my arms for climbing, but I pressed on. The pain got high enough to squeeze a little sweat onto my forehead, but being familiar with what real pain felt like, I could easily put this pain into context and almost ignore it.

It was not my best climb. The truth is, I was a sad reflection of the climber I had been. The mojo was just not there. There were none of the old fluid movements; it was just a bunch of herky-jerky moves. Vertical stumbling. There was none of the old singular focus on the work. Instead there was a focus on making sure I didn't fall. It was "scared climbing" pure and simple, not confident climbing, and any climber will tell you that scared climbing is the worst kind. You make bad decisions. You burn up energy. You focus on one move at a time instead of planning ahead and stringing together several moves to get where you want to be.

Forever and a day after I'd first put my hands on the rock I reached the anchor 40 feet up and clipped in. The easy part was over.

I had to thread the rope through the anchor and then unclip from it so Jeff could lower me. I sweated and fumbled my way through it until the moment of truth came. And that's where I froze.

The last time I'd looked at an anchor like this, I'd seen it streaking away from me. I had a full flashback to that moment of falling. I could see the complete detail of the anchor again, the webbing, the colors, everything. And here I was again, about to put my trust in the same system. All I had to do was sit back in the harness and let go. Jeff and the rope would take care of the rest. Thousands of people do it in climbing gyms every day. But I just couldn't.

Let go, I tried to tell myself. *Let go, let go, let go.* My hands were like vise grips on the anchor.

I could have just climbed down. There was no law requiring me to be lowered on belay, and it was a very easy downclimb. In a couple of minutes it'd be over. No harm, no foul.

"I got you, Craig. Nice job!"

It was Jeff, calling from below, trying to be reassuring.

I stared down, thinking about picking my way back down to the ground and knowing in my heart that I shouldn't do it that way. I needed to trust the system. If I didn't trust it today, now, I might not ever. And I'd know for sure that I could never climb again.

I called down to Jeff, who assured me again that he had me. I twisted my neck around and looked back at him, needing to see for myself. He was tied in and paying attention, just like he was supposed to be.

Right next to the climbing wall there's a small hillside. It's easily walkable; someone could make their way up it and be at the same height as a climber at the top of the rock wall, and only a few yards away. Cyndy had perched herself there, not talking, just watching.

I turned from Jeff and looked over to her. My wife. My partner. The woman who had waited for this day as much as I had.

She smiled.

And I let go.

The rope stretched and creaked as I dangled for a second in the harness, starting to make a lazy turn, until Jeff gently released the tension on his end and I took a slow elevator ride to the ground.

Inch by inch I descended until my shoes touched the dirt and I could stand. I took a deep breath, relief filling my whole body just as the air filled my lungs. The harness had held. I was safe. I had climbed again. I was also very happy to be done.

Cyndy ran down the hill to join Mayah in giving me an excited hug and asking me how it felt. It was a strange feeling. The gigantic question mark that had been hanging over my head was supposed to be gone now, but it wasn't. The experience had not been what I'd expected. It should have been fun, but it really wasn't. It left me feeling perplexed. Was I a climber again or not? I really didn't know.

Cyndy and I talked more about it that night. I told her honestly that I hadn't enjoyed it. Climbing had been one of the few things in my life where I just understood how everything worked. Not this time. This time it was like I didn't know anything anymore. As I drifted off to sleep, I was still confused, but there was one thing I was certain about. I was willing to keep trying.

***

As I continued to heal and get more active, the biggest question I had to grapple with is one that people still ask me today, years later. Why in the world would I even consider going back to the "dangerous" sport that by all rights should have killed me?

I asked myself that question for a long time after the accident. At first I tried to retreat to the statistics and remind myself that millions of us risk our lives every day just by getting in the car. That rationalization never really worked for me though. There are times in our lives we have to get in the car. Climbing, on the other hand, is always an elective.

Why in the world would I even consider going back to the "dangerous" sport that by all rights should have killed me?

The real truth was that I'd made climbing a part of my DNA. Ever since I was twenty-one years old, if people asked me who I was, invariably one of the first words to come out of my mouth was "climber." I'd never done much sports-wise as a kid; my brother had been the football star while I'd been good at art. When I discovered climbing I found my athletic medium and I jumped in as far as I could. Ice, big walls, traditional ("trad") bouldering; if there was a way to get vertical on it, I tried it. I'd never experienced anything where I'd been so "in the moment," undistracted by anything. And I was never sad when I was climbing. Never once.

When I'd climb, even if it was just bouldering for half an hour, I'd feel great in a way that went beyond how I was internally. It gave me this wonderful feeling of grace and movement, and I'd get into that mode of concentration where there was nothing else, only the rock and making my way forward. There are very few times you can be so focused on what you're doing that you shake off all the other distractions and stresses of life and nothing else seeps through. Climbing did that for me. It's a sport that forces you to pay attention and keep your focus because if you don't, as my own experience had shown, you'll get hurt.

I once heard someone, an English climber as I recall, say climbing is one of those things that when you're doing it, it might not be fun or at times even seems stupid. But later, when you think about it, you realize that in those moments you were also at your most alert, most dialed in to everything that was going on around you, and performing at your peak level.

I can understand how, at first blush, anyone would think my interest in going back to climbing was insane. Trust me, there were many times I felt exactly the same. But the one inescapable truth was that I liked how climbing made me feel and I didn't want to remove that from my life. And I'd remember that the whole purpose behind cutting my leg off had been centered on a better quality of life. If I didn't pursue that better life, then it was all for nothing. If my sanity was really the central question, the fact was if I didn't at least try to go back to climbing, that would be crazier.

Of course, that was all well and good if it was all about me. The real question I had to ask myself was whether I really believed God had saved me, and restored me, just so I could go put myself at risk again.

Some people, as a rationale for not getting involved in a church fellowship, like to say "nature is my cathedral." Or, one of my favorites, "I'd rather be outside thinking about God than sitting in church and thinking about being outside." I could certainly identify with that. It was easy to see God in every aspect of climbing because I'd come across the most amazing things. Once, at this little bouldering spot, I peeked into a crack and saw a little bat had made a home in it. Another time I was in Yosemite, a couple thousand feet up, and I came across this patch of perfect little pink flowers, just tucked into a nook in the middle of nowhere with nothing but stone for nourishment. I'd see things like that and just take a moment to be awed. And grateful. I was seeing something few else on Earth would see and, more's the pity, most could never fully appreciate what they'd missed as they sped purposefully through their lives. It was as if God had left behind a small calling card just to remind me He was still there.

Of course, I knew I could go on a hike in the woods and have the same kind of experience. I didn't need climbing to feel close to God. What I needed was to feel that God wanted me to climb.

There was no doubt God had saved me for a reason and I knew better than to squander the gift He'd given me.

I didn't take the question lightly. There was no doubt God had saved me for a reason and I knew better than to squander the gift He'd given me. I thought back through everything that had led to this point and one conclusion just kept coming back over and over. It was impossible not to see God's hand in everything that had directed me back to climbing: the number of believers around me throughout my rescue, the miraculous way my body had healed, the people who came into my life and showed me who I could be, all in the perfect order and all at the perfect times.

I had never prayed that God would get me back into climbing. I had never pushed for it. Up until the amputation I had, in fact, begun to accept that I would never climb again and was trying to figure out what that meant for who I was going to be for the rest of my life. But God kept opening doors and I simply walked through. That's really what it came down to. I don't presume to speak for God or to know

His mind. I just know that if He had thrown up any roadblocks to climbing again, I would have stopped.

Beyond all the emotional and spiritual questions, however, there were also the practical ones. For starters, there was no way I could be a

serious climber with an ordinary "walking foot." That might be good for quick and easy climbs with the kids, but for the harder stuff I needed something much different.

I was still seeing Joe a couple times a month. Even with as much as he knew about how to get amputees active again, with me we were in something of a gray area. Just looking at the numbers, less than one half of one percent of the U.S. population is comprised of amputees. Less than half of them are what could be called active. An even smaller percentage are lower leg amputees, and only a fraction of those could be called athletes. By the time you narrow it down to lower leg amputees who are advanced-level rock climbers, you're talking about a U.S. market of maybe a dozen people. That translated to a very distinct lack of so-called industrial knowledge on how to make a workable foot for me, and prescribed a path that was going to involve a lot of trial and error.

By six months after the surgery I was a regular at the climbing gym again, and some of the old mojo had started to come back. I was also climbing outside, mostly bouldering to build my endurance and to get a feel for how the foot would play on the rock. And to learn to trust it. I was regaining that feeling of working through the problems and solving the puzzles that would get me to the next handhold and eventually to the top. And I realized that if that was all starting to come back, then I did still love this sport after all, at some level anyway.

How far I'd be able to go was a matter of many questions, but my prosthesis was the most glaring. At the gym I'd been making it work with one of the first factory-designed prosthetics Joe had suggested. I'd wanted something with a shock on it, but the problem was that what the foot gave me in flexibility at the "ankle," it cost me in terms of stability. The material was just too flexible. It was hard enough trying to navigate up a wall with a foot that couldn't actually feel the toeholds, but whenever I'd put my right foot on a hold it felt like I was standing on the end of a diving board. That was a little disconcerting; the last thing you want when you're halfway up a pitch is to feel like you're about to bounce yourself right off it. I tried to improvise, and even wore the foot backward one time, but to no avail.

When I saw Joe again, I told him we needed to design a foot. I think he liked the challenge of that. He shoved all the papers on his desk aside and gave me his full attention.

"Okay," he said. "Tell me what you're thinking."

"I need something that's going to be much more stable. I need to be able to put my weight on the toe and not have any flex in the foot at all."

Joe nodded. "Chrome-moly. The same stuff they make mountain bikes out of. That's what we need."

Over the next hour or so, we hunched over his desk and sketched out the rest of the design until Joe had something he could work with to make a prototype.

I was psyched. On paper, it really looked like this thing was going to work, and when I locked into the real thing for the first time three weeks later, I was all but convinced we'd hit upon the right solution.

I glued climbing rubber on the bottom to give me a little more traction and at the first second I started going up the wall I was ecstatic. It had exactly the feel I wanted.

I'd made it up all of about four feet when the whole front end snapped off and I crashed to the ground.

Fortunately, I was in an outside area and all alone. I can only imagine the shocked gasps of horror if I'd been in a climbing gym, not to mention the red-hot embarrassment I'd have felt.

I was still a bit shocked when it happened, of course. There was literally a great big snapping sound, and I was on the ground.

I called Joe who, not surprisingly, said we needed to make the foot again out of something harder. Titanium.

This was 2004, the post-9/11 world. You couldn't just go out and buy titanium.

All we needed was one 12 x 12 piece, but Joe must have spent the better part of a week trying to track it down. When we finally found a company that could get it, the price was almost enough to trigger a mild panic. Almost.

We also needed someone who could weld it. In yet another example of the stream of signs that God was making it easy for me to climb again, there was a guy at my own church, Jon Hanson, who through his work at Colorado Iron & Metal had the tools and equipment to do the job.

I'll never forget walking into the place to get the work done. It had the look and feel of a large recycling center. Hardly the kind of place where you'd expect to see the birth of cutting-edge prosthetic manufacturing. None of that mattered. He got the job done perfectly.

The hardness of the titanium, however, presented a new problem. I had a workable foot, but to make it suitable for climbing I needed to be able to glue rubber on it. Titanium has no pores, offering the glue nothing to grab on to, and I couldn't do anything to rough up the surface. The titanium always won out over whatever material or tool I tried.

Finding myself at a stalemate again, I started calling around, and finally found a place called Rock & Resoles in Boulder. I talked to the owner, Eric, and while he didn't have any immediate answers he knew what I was getting at and persuaded me to send him the foot.

Almost two weeks went by and I began to wonder if he'd melted the foot down and sold the metal. My worries were put to rest when Eric finally called.

"I've been staring at your foot for a week," he said. "It's been sitting here on my desk. I think I can solve your problem, but I need to change the shape just a little bit. Is that okay?

I wasn't thrilled with the idea, but as Eric explained what he wanted to do I got on board. Plus, I really had nothing to lose. If I couldn't put rubber on it, the foot wasn't much use for climbing anyway.

In the end, he'd had to drill little pockets in the metal and then super heated it to actually bond the metal to the rubber. I still don't know exactly how he made it all work, but it was phenomenal right from the get-go. At the climbing gym I was tentative on it for the first half hour, gradually putting more faith in it until I began deliberately trying to break the thing. It was indestructible. I could climb on it, jam it in cracks and bear down on it with all I had.

I felt absolutely solid on it. And all I could think was, *Oh my gosh. Freedom.*

If it had one problem it was that out in the world, where the real rocks are a little rougher than the gym, the rubber would get completely chewed up in a single day of climbing and would have to be replaced. For this, Eric charged me exactly seven dollars.

I was back.

10

LURKING FEAR

In September 2005, my fortieth birthday rolled around. I'd been climbing regularly with Cyndy for three months, still tentative, but taking small steps forward. I was back into the swing of things—maybe not performing at my peak, but I was certainly well past the feelings of fear that had plagued me at first.

To welcome me to middle age, Cyndy surprised me with a trip to Arco, Italy. Arco is a huge climbing center in Europe with a climber's buffet of cliffs right outside of town. Most of the climbs are also easily accessible, which makes them attractive for someone who's struggling with basic walking and might not be in the mood for a tough hike. Arco also perpetuates Italy's reputation for being a place of epic scenery and romantic flavor, but without the crowds.

I'd known for a while that I would be a climber again, at some level, but until we left for Arco that level had still been pretty basic. I was doing more technical climbs, yes, but I was still only top roping or, basically, climbing second instead of lead climbing.

Lead climbing is inherently more dangerous than any other climbing, except free soloing, which involves the use of no ropes or safety equipment at all. To lead climb means going up first and putting all the equipment in the cracks and other features that would then serve to protect me if I fell. Even with those safeties in place, if you fall as a lead climber, you can get some serious air time, because you fall as far as the length of rope between you and your last piece of equipment, and then the length of that rope again until the safety kicks in. If I lead climbed and fell, I'd fall twice as far and twice as hard and not stop until I "took a whipper," which in climbing parlance describes the moment when the rope pulls tight and yanks you to a stop. (Hitting the ground, by the way, is called "augering." There's no shortage of good gallows humor in the climbing world.)

Despite the gastric distress that came with the idea of climbing lead, I really wanted to know what it felt like to do it again. Arco seemed like a good place to try, and physically I was ready.

I chose a climb that should have been easy, but as I started up ahead of Cyndy, fear took me in its cold hands and squeezed. Just like that day at Wild Iris, I was climbing scared, only this time I was closer to petrified because, in my mind, I'd decided my body was still too fragile. The hard truth of my physical condition blared in my mind and the doubts slithered in. My back was fused, making it hard to bend and stretch and forcing me to change how I climbed. I had a fake foot that couldn't feel the ground, so simply walking was a matter of faith, yet here I was climbing up a rock, needing my "toes" to hold on to small nubbins of rock that I couldn't feel at all. Who knew how long they'd hold or, more frightening, who knew when my metal foot would slip off the rock and send me rushing toward the ground. All I could think of was how I was going to fall and get wrecked again.

I practically shook myself off the wall, and even when I pulled it together enough to keep moving I over-gripped every hold, and fought the rock instead of working with it.

Cyndy could tell I was scared. Half of Italy could probably tell I was scared. Climbing scared was bad enough when I was only top roping; in that situation I was only really making it harder on myself. But in lead position, climbing scared could mean all kinds of bad things for me and the other climbers. I could fumble equipment and drop it on them. I could, in a moment of haste, place a piece of equipment wrong and put safety at risk. Every mistake is magnified, frustrating, and leads to even more mistakes.

Cyndy shouted up encouragement.

"You got this!" she'd tell me often, in between telling me to just relax, look around, and take in the beauty of the place.

Normally all that would have worked, but that day none of it worked in the slightest.

Later, safe again on level ground, we talked about what had happened. I told her it had not been a fun climb, but it had been a good experiment. I'd wanted to figure out what kind of climber I was going to be. If I was just going to be limited to bouldering and top roping for the rest of my life, I wanted to know.

The fear stayed with me for most of that year, although it was in varying degrees. Some days there was none, other days it was overwhelming. I just wasn't ready to fully trust everything I had trusted about climbing before. I had the knowledge I needed, but I was questioning everything. There were some bolts I could clip into and I knew they could hold up my truck, but I'd question whether they could hold me. I'd ask myself if I could really trust the rope, or the webbing, or the carabineers.

> **The fear stayed with me for most of that year, although it was in varying degrees. Some days there was none, other days it was overwhelming.**

Baby step by baby step I overcame those little fears, until I was confronted once again by the question of whether I was ever going to lead climb again. I'd once thought that I could just top rope through the rest of my life, but as I began to think more about what I really enjoyed about climbing, it was the mental challenge, and the focus climbing required. I liked figuring out all the variables that came with lead climbing, and those were all but extinct in top roping. I could never again enjoy climbing as much as I had in the past if I just settled into the routine again.

What nagged at me most of all was that I didn't want fear to be the reason I stopped. Once I knew my body was up to the rigors of it, I just needed to get my head together so I could move forward, not just with climbing but with life in general. If I let fear stop me in this area of my life, then it would probably gain footholds in a lot of other areas as well. I think once you cave in to it once, it's much easier to say "no" again and again, and I didn't want to be that person.

As I wrestled with that, I realized there was only one way I could ever really trust the system again, move beyond the fear, and become the climber I thought I was really meant to be. But that required something I didn't want to think about. I had to let the system save me. I had to fall again.

I've always known falling is a part of climbing but not knowing what a fall might do to me made me a very tentative climber. Maybe that was for the best at first; I may not have climbed well, but at least

I climbed smart, and over time I got my body back into shape. As I got more fit and the muscle memory came back I felt stronger. That helped with my confidence and I could push myself harder again. It took almost a year of climbing after the Arco trip for me to feel like I was ready to climb lead again. And when I did fall for the first time, it was insignificant in every way but one.

It was a tiny fall, maybe all of five feet, at a place called Shelf Road. I was sport climbing (meaning the bolts are all in place already) and I was maybe three or four feet above the last bolt. Without warning, I just popped off a hold and fell. It happened so suddenly and was over so quickly that I never even had a chance to worry that I could fall, or to realize what was happening until I was hanging from the rope. Nothing broke, nothing hurt, and after taking a moment or two to soak in the enormity of what had just happened, I went on and finished the route.

What that fall did for me as a climber, however, changed me. As I thought about it more and more, I realized I could trust the system again after all. And just like any relationship, when it's built on trust and you can fully commit to it, it grows in ways you didn't know were possible. Suddenly I was able to stretch myself as a climber, both mentally and physically. It didn't mean I could take stupid risks, but at least I could be a more confident climber. Things that before may have seemed like folly could be doable. I think that's why, when I opened a magazine and saw an ad for the Extremity Games, I decided to go for it.

I hadn't spent much time looking at magazines targeted at "the disabled," but there was one, called *In Motion,* that was a hybrid sporting/if-you-want-to-be-active-again-here-are-some-things-you-can-do kind of thing. I came across the Extremity Games ad halfway through. The double meaning was not lost on me as I noticed the picture had a guy on a motorcycle and another guy who was a climber. It dawned on me that this could be an objective, something to focus on and train for, and really get me back into peak climbing shape. I picked the magazine up and brought it over to Cyndy.

"I think I'm going to do this," I said, pointing at the ad.

"Okay, good," she said. "You always work best when you have a goal."

She knows me so well.

I went to the website and signed up that day for the speed climbing competition, the only competition they were featuring that year. I couldn't help noticing that the date of the games was July 21—the fourth anniversary of my accident.

That gave me a solid five months to train, which was good because I didn't know the first thing about speed climbing, beyond what I'd seen when I watched the X Games on TV. An iconic climber by the name of Hans Florine pretty much owned the sport. I knew he'd written a book on it, but as I was on his website looking for it, I saw that I could send him an email.

Who knew if he ever actually read emails that came from his site, of course, but I thought I'd give it a shot. I banged out a short note telling him my story and asking if he'd be willing to give me a few pointers. He emailed me back almost instantly.

"Here's my cell number," he wrote. "I want you to call me."

I kind of panicked. Hans Florine had always been something of a climbing hero to me. Now he'd just given me his cell number.

For the first fifteen minutes of our conversation he just asked me questions, trying to feel out where I was mentally and physically. We spoke for about forty-five minutes. He gave me all kinds of good tips on speed climbing and then he asked if I had ever climbed in Yosemite. I had climbed on El Capitan back in 1995. We'd done a route called Triple Direct that took us five days.

"Why don't you come out to Yosemite in June," he said. "I have a place there—you can stay with us. Your competition is in July, so train hard, come out in June and we'll climb El Capitan in a day together. I don't think an amputee has ever climbed El Cap in a day before."

"This June?" I asked, like a third grader who just found out his report was due tomorrow.

Hans had said it so casually and matter-of-factly, I thought he was kidding.

"Yes, this June," he said, like he really was talking to a third grader.

We made some tentative plans right there on the phone. I kept thinking about how this was the climbing equivalent of being invited to play basketball with Michael Jordan, and Hans's confidence was infectious. If I kept up with my training and came out to Yosemite in June, we would absolutely get it done.

El Capitan is a 3,000-foot vertical wall and one of the largest granite monoliths in the world. It's a very popular destination for hard-core climbers. The typical ascent takes anywhere from three to five days. That's fully experienced, able-bodied climbers carrying full backpacks, sleeping gear, the works.

Cyndy had gone out while I was on the phone and when she came home a while later, she could see I was in a bit of a state. When she asked me what was up, I told her the truth. Hans Florine had just insisted that I come to Yosemite in June and climb El Capitan with him in a single day.

I wasn't sure what kind of response I'd get. Cyndy had always been my greatest cheerleader, but I thought this might just be a bit much.

"You're going to do it, right?"

"I kind of told him yes . . ."

"Good. We'll go out there together. We'll all go."

It was that easy. But for the next several weeks, even as I trained harder and harder to prepare, I questioned my sanity. I'd simply reached out to Hans for some tips on how to climb faster, and now, four years after the accident—four years after not even being able to sit up on my own—I'd signed on to do a climb no one on Earth had ever done before.

I convinced myself that things had happened too easily for God's hand not to be in it. Doors I hadn't even knocked on simply opened and I walked through; that was it. I'd think about how God always has things in motion that I don't even know about or couldn't possibly comprehend until much later. I chose to believe that this was something God was leading me into, and therefore He would also lead me out.

Though it may sound like it, I was not trying to justify the decision to go. In fact, something I never told Cyndy until much later was that I was pretty sure I was going to get really wrecked again, or killed, on the El Cap attempt. I knew realistically that was unlikely—as odd as it sounds to most people, climbing really is a safe sport, when it's done safely—but I also knew what the risk was now, in a way I'd never been able to comprehend before the accident.

That forced me to ask myself why I would go through with it. I had never tried anything like it before, even with a good body.

At the center of the onion that was my brain on this was the need to know if it really could be done. And if El Cap actually did chew me up and spit me out, at least I'd go doing something I loved.

I had Cyndy's support. I'd justified it to myself. I prayed that God would keep me safe. And with all that, I was in a good place . . . until I slipped up and told my parents what I was planning.

I hadn't told my parents that I'd been doing any climbing at all. I'd planned to let them in on my big secret after I got back from Yosemite but, once again, my focus got a little lax.

I talk to my mom about once a week, like any good son . . . and one day in May as we were chatting she threw out some dates for getting together. She was listing a couple dates in June and without thinking I just blurted out that I'd be in Yosemite then.

I knew what I'd done instantly, so I just kept talking, trying to cover it up. Mom was silent on the other end of the phone. If you know my mom, you know she's never silent. My diversion plan was failing, and I knew it.

She patiently let me finish jabbering and then asked, "What was that you said? About Yosemite?"

I could no more put anything past her at age forty than I could at four.

"Oh, yeah, the family and I are going out to Yosemite."

There was a short pregnant pause, as if she was giving me the chance to fess up, before she spoke again.

"For what? You're not going to climb Yosemite . . ."

"Oh, Mom," I said. "Yosemite is a national park. You don't climb Yosemite. You climb Half Dome or El Capitan."

It was about as pathetic an attempt at deflection as I'd ever made, and it really set her off.

"You know exactly what I mean," she said in a tone I remembered only too well. "I'm going to get your father."

She slammed the phone on the table as I relived my childhood.

Oh man, I thought. *She really is going to get my dad.* It was hard not to smirk at all of this.

I heard his footsteps coming and the phone chunked as he grabbed it.

"What's this your mom's telling me."

It's amazing how a question can sometimes sound like anything *but* a question.

Mom picked up the extension. Both of them were livid, asking how I could be so foolish, so reckless; what I was thinking. I gave them the whole safety speech I'd been telling myself for weeks.

"I'll be as safe as I possibly can," I told them. "Hans is one of the best climbers in the world."

But they'd been there in the hospital with me. They'd seen for themselves what could happen and as any parent knows, seeing your child hurt like that takes something from you. Almost more than you can afford to give.

In the end I had to play the I'm-a-grownup-and-I-make-my-own-decisions card.

"This is something I really think I can do," I said. "It's something I want to do. Cyndy and the kids are going to be there to support me. I'm doing this, and that's just the way it is."

They wanted to know the instant I was back on the ground. That's not to say they supported my decision in the end. We talked for several more minutes and it was not an encouraging conversation. I hung up with an air of angst hanging over me.

It wasn't really the return to climbing that was the issue, although that was certainly at the core. They just didn't understand why I had to ramp it up so much. Why go from fairly basic climbing right into something that people were saying simply couldn't be done?

That question had never occurred to me before, but it hung with me over the next several weeks and I'd ask myself, *Why* am *I doing this?* I'd never even thought of such a challenging climb before I'd called Hans, and I'd committed right away, without even thinking or praying about it. *Do I really need to ramp it up this far, this fast? It's one thing to do something I've never done before, but to try something no one has ever done before? Isn't that a bit much?*

In the end, I always kept coming back to yes, I want to do this, even as I felt that it really was a bad idea. I told myself I'd just do it one length of rope (one pitch) at a time. I'd just take it all in 200-foot chunks, and not think about it as a whole. Once again, when the big picture was just too much to take in all at once, being able to focus on the smaller pieces in isolation was a huge help.

Physically I was feeling really good. I was training five days a week and climbing some really big stuff, getting in as many pitches as I could. Mentally I was still pretty sure I was going to get hurt again. Don't ask me why. I just kept it to myself. I needed Cyndy to believe I was as confident as I appeared. The most I did was to get her opinion on whether she thought I was ready.

"It doesn't matter what I think," she'd say. "You're ready. You're going."

My confidence was not helped when, as we started the trip, we missed our flight out. We had the whole family with us, as well as a couple of friends, including Cyndy's maid of honor, and I'd been pretty wound up all the way to the airport. It was my usual syndrome—I was getting all tight inside and fidgety because I just wanted to get started on the climb. This particular bout of anxiety was laced with streaks of self-doubt, despite the fact that I'd trained my tail off. Worse, instead of the usual twenty-four-hour cycle, I'd been obsessing about this climb for three months. I really wished I could just chill out, but I knew that until I put my hands and feet on that wall and pulled/pushed up for the first time, I was going to have to roll with the twisted-up gut. Thus, it was not helpful to realize that I still had a thousand miles to go, and my plane was gone.

Of course, it wasn't an insurmountable problem. Planes fly from Colorado to California about every hour, and by the time we boarded our new flight I was much calmer. I'd stopped anticipating the climb and started to just focus on the experience. And maybe that's exactly what God needed me to do.

In the end all of us had to take three separate planes to arrive in San Francisco at the same relative time, but we made it and drove from there to Hans's house in west Yosemite. Hans himself wasn't there yet, he was off somewhere doing Hans things, but that had been part of the plan. I was able to take a few days and get comfortable in the house and, more importantly, get comfortable with the local climbing. I couldn't just show up and climb The Capitan—Yosemite climbing has its own special feel and you have to get into the groove of it. The granite there is described as similar to something that's just come out of a pottery kiln because of its smoothness. Sometimes the rock has a nice warm feeling with thousands of tiny little features that your feet can just glom right onto. Other times it's like marble, slick and polished. When the sun heats it up the climbing rubber on your shoes won't stick to it at all and you have to use your arms more than your legs to climb. That's the opposite of how it's supposed to be done—climbing is mostly a leg sport—so it takes a little time to wrap your head around that.

Having a couple days to get acclimated was the best therapy for my anxiety. By the time Hans arrived I was absolutely psyched to get going.

A day before the climb, Hans and I met in El Capitan's meadow and talked through the whole climb. We were taking on a route aptly named "Lurking Fear," and looking up from the meadow it was easy to follow its course almost all the way up. We'd be speed climbing the whole way, switching lead every two hours (a tactic called swinging leads) and carrying everything we'd need on our own backs.

When I'd first learned of speed climbing I, like most people, assumed it meant climbing at a sprint pace. That's actually true in some competition contexts, but not in terms of what Hans does.

In normal climbing, the leader climbs up a pitch, gets to the anchor and belays the second climber up to the anchor position. The belay itself might take fifteen minutes or so, and once both climbers are together, it can take another ten minutes to re-rack and organize gear, and move on. To go up 3,000 feet, we'd be doing twenty-two 200-foot pitches. If we were climbing traditionally, the belays alone would have taken more than seven hours. That's in part why traditional climbing up something like El Cap is also called "vertical camping." The belays and transitions take so much time that you have to plan on it taking more than a day, or at least you have to plan on stopping at some point before you hit the summit. That means you need to bring a whole bunch of extra gear with you—sleeping bag, portaledge, extra food, and other equipment. It all gets stuffed into a huge duffel bag, not so lovingly called a *pig*. A more fitting name there could not be, because once the climbers reach their anchor, that bag has to be hauled up by hand at a great cost of energy and an even greater cost of time. It's a little ironic—the gear you bring in preparation for an extended time on the wall is actually one of the main reasons the climb takes so long.

In speed climbing, however, there's none of that. There's no pig, because no extra gear is brought along. Enough food and water for one day is carried in a small pack. When the lead climber reaches the end of a pitch, he fixes a line to an anchor, calls down to announce the line is fixed, and keeps going until he runs out of gear or reaches an agreed upon stopping point.

In its purest form, speed climbing is just traditional climbing with all the dead time removed. Unlike the competition variety, true speed climbing is not about sprinting up the rock or leaping from hold to hold. It's just constant, unrelenting movement upward.

Hans and I agreed we'd climb in two-hour chunks, then break quickly for food and water and to switch lead. We talked through every detail, right down to how we each liked to wear our harness and orient our gear (clips outward versus clips inward), so when it was time to switch, the transitions would be seamless and eliminate minutes that could easily add up to hours.

I was once again impressed by Hans's style and his amazing ability to make even the grandest things seem so very casual. Here we were standing in front of the largest monolith in America, the one Mayah had looked at earlier and declared there was no way we were going to climb it in a day, and he started chatting about breakfast. He just gave off this vibe that accomplishing incredible things was totally normal for him, and I found that I could easily be cool with that. That was the moment when I clicked over. The anxiety disappeared and a fresh dose of confidence pushed in. I *was* physically ready for this. I *did* know what I was doing. This *was* going to be a lot of fun for me. I went to bed that night relaxed for the first time in weeks.

That's not to say I slept well, of course. The mere act of going to bed was hardly worth the effort with the alarm set for 2:00 in the morning. My usual pre-climb nervousness trickled back, but more than that I knew that no matter what the outcome, I was going to be a different person when I got back to the house.

Hans wanted to beat the heat so he set a start time of 6:00 AM. It was a half-hour drive into the valley and then about an hour's walk to the base. Cyndy came with us—she was jazzed about seeing El Cap up close, but also wanted to be as much help and encouragement to me as she could. The hike to the base involved a lot of uphill climbing and scrambling to get on the ledges that led to Lurking Fear. Cyndy carried my pack for me the whole way so I'd have as much energy as possible for the climb. That really meant a lot.

We got to our launch area a little after 5:00. It was still dark, so we actually had time to eat a little bit and wait around until there was enough light to climb. As we tied in, Hans didn't stand on ceremony. He just said, "Okay, three, two, one," then hit his timer and blasted off up the first pitch. Cyndy and I watched him for a few minutes until it was my turn to follow. I told her I loved her and, with one final deep breath, attacked the rock.

I didn't even see Hans for the first hour. He's that fast. His whole first block was 400 feet, but he did 500 feet in less than two hours. That's absolutely flying.

I was feeling good as I joined him at the anchor and we switched gear so I could lead. We had a quick chat and off I went.

Hans was incredibly supportive and encouraging as I led. I already knew how much faster he could climb than I, and I'd been a little worried about whether I'd be able to move fast enough for him. It was never an issue. He shouted up encouragement and I realized I was having a really good time. I wasn't worried at all about my RSD kicking in. I knew that the constant motion and working of the muscles would keep it at bay. I didn't feel stiff or sore or uncomfortable. I won't go as far as to say I was "one with the rock"; I wasn't, but I'd get to spots where I could see a good crack or a very manageable series of handholds and I'd get overjoyed. I could do this.

When we were about halfway up I finally stopped for a brief moment to look around. As usual I'd been completely focused on the climb, but I'd just come up around a corner and seen the whole valley below me.

Think about where you are, I told myself. *You're back in Yosemite, climbing El Capitan with freaking* Hans Florine, *and looking over one of the most beautiful places in the world. Don't let this moment pass unnoticed.*

And I didn't. It was a real feel-the-presence-of-God moment where I could be so incredibly thankful to be there, enjoying this experience and realizing how far God had brought me.

I grabbed my walkie-talkie and radioed down to Cyndy, who I knew would be in the meadow below with the kids by now. I'd worn a bright red shirt and at the moment I radioed, they could all see me. I was nothing more than a red speck on the wall, but it was enough. The kids wanted to know if I could see them down in the meadow (not a prayer) and we all chatted about

> It was a real feel-the-presence-of-God moment where I could be so incredibly thankful to be there, enjoying this experience and realizing how far God had brought me.

how the climb was going. I told them all the truth. I was really having fun.

I told Cyndy that I loved her and signed off. As I did, Hans—who knows El Cap like it's his own playground—shouted up.

"Another eight hours and we'll be done and off!"

That really psyched me up. Eight hours may sound like a long time, but I knew it was going to pass by really fast.

We plugged right along until we were just two pitches below the top. There's a large cave there—it was a perfect place to drop the packs and climb unencumbered to the top.

Hans led for the final pitch. There's a small tree at the summit, and the tradition is to touch it to make the climb official before starting back down. We high-fived at the tree and shook hands. Our official time was fourteen hours. I'd just become the first amputee to climb up El Capitan in less than one day.

Of course, the climb isn't actually over until you get down, and we had four hours of rappelling ahead of us. Moment over.

It was early evening as we got back to the cave and we knew we'd be rappelling in the dark before it was done. That makes finding the anchors on the way down a little bit of a challenge. They're usually right below you somewhere, but even in broad daylight you kind of have to hunt for them.

I had a brand new headlamp clamped to my helmet and it was shining brightly into the darkness by the time of our sixth rappel. Hans was below me and had just yelled up that he was at the anchor. I leaned over to take a look down and heard a sharp plastic snap as the clip on my headlamp pinched itself off my helmet. I watched it tumbling over and over in freefall, down into the darkness.

My first worry was that it was going to hit Hans, but I could mark where he was by his headlamp and saw instantly that there was no danger of that. Then, suddenly I could see how the rest of this brief scenario was going to play out and, bummed as I was about my brand new headlamp, I smirked.

The headlamp rushed silently past Hans, the circle-like beacon vanishing into the night below. As I watched, Hans's own headlamp froze in place. He had no way of knowing whether or not I was still actually wearing the light as it plummeted into the black.

There was a moment of silence, and then a question.

"Craig?"

I purposefully waited a few extra seconds before I answered, laughing.

Hans got my little joke.

"Yeah . . . ," he said. "That's not so funny . . ."

I gave him a grin he couldn't see and told him I just couldn't resist. And that he'd have to find all the anchors for the rest of the descent.

That turned out to be not entirely true. Before long, a big beautiful full moon came out and lit up the rock like silver. We were making good time, but I told myself not to get sloppy. That last part of the descent is often the most dangerous because you're at your most tired, and your thoughts drift ahead to warm meals and warmer beds, instead of staying focused on the work. And by about the third hour of rappelling I was tired. Really tired. My hips hurt from being in a harness all day. My neck, which had been facing the sun all day, was crispy. I was chaffed and scratched, and it became just rappel after rappel after rappel until mentally I got to the point of, *Okay, this can be done now.*

I'd lost track of how many rappels we'd done. I knew we had to do about eighteen and I knew we were well past halfway, but that was it until, finally, I could look down and see the ground. Forty-five minutes to go.

When we finally touched down I was too thrashed to even enjoy being done. I just shrugged off my gear and at last allowed my brain to come down a notch or two on the alert scale. That felt good.

Hans has a little tradition he likes to do after every El Cap climb. We walked a few yards over to a nearby stream and plunged our hands in, up to the elbows. Next we did the same with our feet. The ice cold water on my abused and swollen muscles was like heaven. I could have just rolled my whole body in and stayed there.

We used the stream to freshen up and it soaked all my soreness away, to the point that as I climbed back into bed at 1:00 AM, twenty-three hours after I'd left it, I was actually giddy. The enormity of what I'd just done had finally hit me like a giant caffeine rush. I was giggling to myself as I pulled up the covers, and I can't say for sure that I slept at all for the next five hours. When the clock read 6:00, I gave up trying and just got up to make a cup of coffee.

Of course, my muscles had all set while I was lying still, and as I tried to walk it was easy to take stock of the punishment I'd administered. My stump was sore. Despite the pads I'd worn, my knees were battered. I couldn't even close my hand into a fist. To say I felt like I'd been hit by a bus doesn't cover it. It was like each part of my body was being hit by separate busses, all at once. I'd taken some of my pain drugs when I'd been at the summit, knowing my back would be throbbing later and trying to soften that blow. I told myself to think about how much worse I'd feel if I hadn't done that.

I called my parents just as I'd promised. They were very relieved, but still not entirely warm to the idea of me climbing again. It wasn't until they saw me on CNN a week or so later that they really understood. The network had been alerted to my accomplishment and wanted to interview me live on the air. It was a very weird experience. After the broadcast they both called, so excited and gushing about how cool it was that I was on CNN. We talked awhile and by the time I hung up I could tell that they were ready to support me in my continued climbing.

As happy as I was to be climbing again, knowing they were behind me made it so much better.

The El Cap climb turned out to be the first in a series of events that launched me into a newfound bit of distinction in the climbing world.

Just a few weeks after Yosemite, as planned, I participated in my first speed climbing competition at the Extremity Games. It was a much different experience than the speed climbing I'd just done. They basically put you in front of a giant Plexiglas wall with holds on it, fire the starting gun, and you huck yourself up it as fast as you can.

Hans had given me some good advice.

"Don't worry about looking at your feet," he told me. "Keep your eyes up, always up, and any time your feet touch something, push off of it. With your hands, it's just grab and pull."

Frankly, it didn't involve a lot of skill or technique. Case in point, the young guy who won had never climbed before in his life. Modesty and good sportsmanship prevent me from saying too much more about that, or how I actually gave the guy some tips earlier in the day or how, had I not missed a hold in the finals, I'd have beaten him and taken the gold instead of the bronze. But I digress . . .

The best part about those games was being in an environment where I was surrounded by fellow athletes, men and women, who were amputees. It was inspiring and a little humbling sometimes, to see how much more some of them had lost than I had. A "flesh wound," is how some of them referred to my leg, and perhaps rightly so. There were athletes missing entire limbs, and sometimes more than one, and they were doing the most amazing things. It was enough to inspire me to come back again.

Over the next three years, I competed in the top roping and bouldering competitions at the Extremity Games—both of which were much better tests of real climbing skill and ability—and took gold medals in both every year. All of a sudden I had sponsors. People wanted to learn from me and were asking for advice. I'd become something of a celebrity in that corner of the world.

And it dawned on me, in a moment of extreme awe and gratitude, that I was living the life I had imagined for myself before the accident. I was a sponsored climber. People were coming to me for advice and tips on climbing. I was winning prize money. I was in every respect a professional climber. And God had made it all happen. Not in the way I'd envisioned it, but in a way that I suddenly realized could do more for His kingdom than I ever had imagined, or could have done on my own. I'd thought that just walking around with a fake leg would be good for starting one-on-one conversations about what God had done, but my success in climbing with a fake leg, from the beginning, created a platform that I never could have had as an "able-bodied" climber.

> **And it dawned on me, in a moment of extreme awe and gratitude, that I was living the life I had imagined for myself before the accident.**

From that point on, the medals and records, as nice as they were, didn't fire me up as much. I knew that in the end, they amounted to nothing of eternal importance. Me talking as a climber wasn't getting anyone to heaven.

I decided it was time to make sure my life was really going the right way.

11

A NEW PURPOSE

The path to reaching more people really started back in 2005, before the El Capitan experience. It was at a time when the last thing I wanted to do was anything that involved public speaking or "ministry."

Of course that's where God, through a co-worker, pushed me. That co-worker, Dave, was constantly on me about doing something to tell my story. He was always asking me why I didn't do this or do that, and I'd be like, *Why don't you just go away?*

He all but insisted that he introduce me to Tina Jacobsen, a speaker's bureau agent, but I resisted mightily. True, I'd learned a lot from my experiences at the Group work camp and the men's breakfast, and from that I knew I could do interviews and talk to one person at a time all day long. But with every fiber of my being I loathed the idea of speaking to a crowd. There were a lot of legitimate-sounding reasons for that.

First of all, my whole livelihood as a photojournalist was based on blending into the background. The better I was at doing that, the better pictures I got. Being in the spotlight was against the grain of everything I'd been trained to do.

Next, I was still dealing with the freak show part of my life. People would seem to think they could gape at me and I wouldn't notice.

Up until the point of getting hurt, I'd seen maybe two amputees, never up close, and until Malcolm's first ill-fated visit I'd never even seen a stump. Now here I was with this thing, and I was starting to expect one of two reactions from people every time I went out in public. One was the "wheelchair look." When it was too much to walk, I'd be out in the chair, where people would see me and literally stop and stare for a moment before moving on. It might last only a second or two, but I could watch it happen and it really bugged me. Cyndy tried to help me understand, telling me that because I was a younger and fit-looking man, the kind that people don't expect to see in a wheelchair, they probably take a moment to wonder what happened to me. They figure something bad must have happened, and as the wheels turn in their brains, everything else shuts down and they just stare.

The other kind of reaction came when I was out of the chair and walking on the prosthetic leg. It seemed to cast some kind of spell on people, because their gaze would freeze on it for a moment, like something was just out of place. Then after a few seconds they'd realize that they were staring, so they'd look up at me and see me making direct eye contact with them. I'd say hi, they'd hi back and then hurry off, looking at my leg the whole way.

Usually I'd just shrug it off and it would be no big deal. Other times, especially on bad pain days when I was already agitated, it would get to me. They'd be so obvious about it, yet think they were being sly, and I'd just want to go over and say, come on, give me a break. I'd always stop before the urge got too great, reminding myself that most people just don't know any better, and but for my own accident I probably would behave no differently. Cyndy would continue to tell me that I just needed to let it go. I used to tell her that I finally understood what it was like for chesty girls to walk down the street.

I should say, in all fairness, that every now and then people surprise me and just walk right up and ask what happened. I remember one lady in particular, a sweet old Baptist grandmother type, who ambled over, touched my arm, and asked me, "Now what did you go and do to yourself?"

I couldn't help but smile, because it's people like her who are interested enough to want to talk to me that I like best. It's an opportunity to connect with people rather than just be a target of stares and gossip.

Beyond all the stealth photography training and sideshow freak insecurities though, the real truth was I felt like standing in front of a crowd somehow conferred a level of knowledge and expertise on me that I did not deserve.

I was just a guy who drove a pickup truck and took pictures for a living. I wasn't prepared to answer faith-based questions or respond to comments about man's spirituality or, by any means, tell someone how they ought to live their life. Right after the accident, when that first writer called and wanted to get my story, I remember my first thought was, "Why?" And as he asked me questions about why I thought God had saved me, my reaction was, "Why would I know?" I couldn't answer that question any more than he could. And as more and more people heard my story, they'd ask the same kind of heavy spiritual questions. They all thought I had something to teach them simply because I had survived.

I felt very much like the blind man who was being harangued by the Pharisees after Jesus healed him on the Sabbath. He didn't know anything about who Jesus was. All he knew were the simple facts. He'd been born blind, and now he could see. I was born a whole person, but now laying in pieces, they thought I knew more.

I shouldn't have survived, but God had saved me. That was all I knew. Beyond that I was just like everyone else, trying to figure it all out as I went along.

Dave and others kept at me, to the point that I really wished they would all just leave me alone. But God was working on me. Every time I tried to put up a wall, He'd knock it down. I had plenty of excuses, but no truly legitimate reason for not stepping out in faith, even if I did it kicking and screaming the whole way.

I called Tina and told her my story. She agreed to represent me while we were still on the phone.

If I'd had any doubts about my credibility as a speaker before, they were doubled once I realized what I'd just committed myself to. A cascade of worries fell on me, all under the banner of trying to figure out what I was going to say to people. I had my outline, but it just felt inadequate. Should I try to incorporate a bunch of Bible verses to underscore the elements of my story? That wasn't me. I felt like even saying "God" and "Jesus" to a crowd of people made me look like an idiot. I tried in vain to figure out what I should try to show people, or what kind of wisdom I was supposed to pass on to them. I could talk to someone over coffee and tell my story, but I was no pastor or spiritual leader. I felt horribly unqualified to try to pass myself off as either, and the people in whose company I now travelled only reinforced my doubts. I'd go to events or see people on TV telling their stories and I'd feel like their faith was so much stronger than mine. I met one speaker who had lost his whole family in a car wreck. Only he had survived and yet he had such a rich relationship with Christ that I felt like he was an apostle. I was actually envious of his faith and felt shallow next to him. Mine was a faith that, despite its resurgence, was still dinged, messed up, and full of holes.

I went home that night and thought about things for a long time. And that's when God gave me the clue that what I really needed to do was shut up.

Mine was a faith that, despite its resurgence, was still dinged, messed up, and full of holes.

I needed to stop blathering to myself that it was all about me, and how spiritually thoughtful or profound I could make myself appear. I needed to take my focus off of who I was, and who I was not, and just let God use me as the person I was.

I found a large measure of comfort when I quieted myself and thought about all the people in the Bible who weren't rabbis or priests, who were less than worthy in their own eyes, and who were reluctant to let themselves be God's messengers. Moses, who killed a man and fled to the desert. Jonah, who heard God call him and tried to run away and hide. David, who betrayed and murdered one of his most faithful soldiers so he could marry the man's wife. The twelve disciples of Jesus, who were not only a ragtag bunch of regular guys and sinners, but were even flawed and weak at the very moments when Jesus needed them most. Even Jesus Himself had once asked that the cup God had prepared might pass from Him.

They had all eventually decided that it was not about them. My situation was no different. This wasn't about how good a speaker I could be or how much insight I had into the mind of God. This was about putting myself out there so people could hear God through me.

I'm not talking about some kind of mystical channeling. What I mean is, all I needed to do was tell my story, in my own words, and in my own style. God's role in it—such as the time the hematoma in my chest just went away overnight in the hospital—would be self-evident. God would do the rest in the hearts and minds of the people who heard me.

When I went to Tina for advice on polishing my speaking a little later, she confirmed everything I'd just realized, and the only suggestion she gave me was to keep it real.

"The power and appeal you have comes from the fact that you're a real person—that's what people want to hear," she said. "Don't try to be a polished performer up there giving them a show. It won't come across as genuine."

That said, as I took steps along the road to being a professional speaker, I realized that while my talk could be somewhat free-flowing, the business side of speaking was a different story. I needed to have a professional back end.

People would call to schedule me to speak and be surprised when it was actually me who answered the phone. They'd ask all kinds of questions: How much would it cost? How long would I speak? Could I send a logo, bio, or other information on letterhead? To which I'd reply, *Um… Er…* and *No, no, and no*, respectively.

Thus, After the Fall Ministry was formed out of necessity. Over time, it came to involve an actual business plan and board of directors, but the focus has always remained on simply telling my story.

With all the back room support in place, and a slightly increased sense of security about my abilities and effectiveness as a speaker, the fact was I still didn't like public speaking. The learning curve for me was pretty steep in terms of trying to relate the accident and my faith to my life, but that was a problem that in the end would work itself out. In the interim, while I didn't like speaking, I quickly fell in love with what happened—and still happens—every time. Because people really did (and do) hear God.

Inevitably when I spoke, someone would come up to me afterward, repeat something back to me, and say how much it meant to them. More often than not, it would be something I didn't remember saying. It was so cool to think I had nothing to do with something that the person had experienced. Something had drawn this individual to come and hear me speak, and as a result God spoke to his heart. People can walk out of a room and forget all about me, but if they can remember what He did for me, and can do for any of us, that's the best thing that can happen. My role in the whole thing is transient.

I never used a stock speech. I developed a list of the main things I wanted to say in my head, but I tried to be a little off-the-cuff so every presentation would be different. That always made me feel a little more in touch with the audience and, I think, created real opportunities for God to work in someone's heart in a way that a stock speech recited the same way over and over again may not have.

I also continued to put a lot of thought into what I wanted people to learn from my experience. I was less concerned about the delivery, but the message still had to come through, and I needed to be clear in my head on what that message was. It had to be more than just my story. It had to be about what my story could mean to them.

I wasn't entirely sure how to achieve that and there was a lot of trial and error before it finally began to crystallize. I made a conscious effort not to pull any punches or try to paint a rosy picture in my talks. I wasn't trying to be depressing, but I knew it would be important to be honest about how things had turned out. I gave audiences a complete inventory of what was still wrong with me physically and what was never going to work right again. I wanted them to know all that so they'd understand what it meant when I told them how I trust God a thousand times more than ever before, despite all that, because I've seen firsthand how He steps up and gets things done.

I wanted them to see how God has been able to use me in spite of (or because of) the broken mess that I was, and that I remain. And in keeping with Tina's advice, I never tried to pass myself off as anything other than a regular guy—someone they could relate to, who had kids, a mortgage, a job, and the ordinary demands of everyday life—yet also someone who went through something horrible and came out on the other side believing that God is the most important part of his life.

As I sculpted and honed my speaking skills, I hoped that if audiences could see that, then maybe it would give them some new perspective on their own lives and whatever they might be dealing with. I wanted them to walk out of the room thinking, *If God can use that guy then maybe He's got something in mind for me too.*

Since no two talks were exactly the same, I also discovered that as I told the story in different ways I'd open my own eyes to different perspectives on it. It became cathartic. I'd be in the middle of a talk and realize something for the first time, working it out in my own head as I spoke. I remember once, when I'd been asked for the umpteenth time why I thought God would allow me to suffer so, I flashed on the fact that my suffering was nothing compared to what Christ had endured. He'd been beaten, whipped, scourged to the point where his skin was all but shredded, and then gone on to endure hours of agony on the cross. I lost a lot, but I kept my life. And I realized that if God Himself would be willing to go through all that pain and suffering and horror in order to save all of us, then I had no reason to think I should be exempt from experiencing my own pain in life. Best of all, I can tell Him about my pain and know that He understands. He's been there.

Something else that began to surface was the simple fact that everyone, and I mean everyone, will go through something hard. Soul-cleansing hard. Like the sifting of wheat, we will all be broken at some point in our lives. I understood that this life was not ever meant to be a perfect situation, and it's so easy to forget that while things are moving along great. Rather than fill me with dread though, my own experience taught me that those soul cleansing times can be true blessings, because it's at those times we experience God in the most profound ways.

> **This life was not ever meant to be a perfect situation, and it's so easy to forget that while things are moving along great.**

I may not have had all the words down perfect, but as more and more of those cathartic moments happened, public speaking became something that was good and healthy for me, and as a result, something I actually began to enjoy. I got more comfortable doing it, I did a better job at it, and I got into a good rhythm. It all came together and, I realize now, by the time I was ready to take the training wheels off of my speaking career, and by the time the reluctance disappeared, it just happened to coincide with the time when my climbing success really exploded.

Actually, I don't see that as a coincidence. I see that as another example of God's timing. I struggled and resisted and grew in my public speaking through all of 2005 and into 2006, so that by the time I climbed El Capitan with Hans, and started winning medals at the Extremity Games, I was fully prepared to tell my story and be excited about doing it. I was the best messenger I could be at the exact moment I was also in the position to tell my story loudest and to the most people.

Public speaking was, however, only the half of it.

As a member of a unique subgroup of society, I had a story I could share with my fellow amputees. My story could be an example. My story could be a form of encouragement. My story could help other people confronting the loss of a limb.

Or so I was willing to believe anyway. When Joe from Quorum Orthopedics first came to me and said it might be good for me to talk to some folks who were going through the same things I had, I pretty much agreed with a shrug. I was no trained counselor; I was just a guy who'd wanted his active life back. But I thought about the people who had been placed in my life, and had helped me so much, and I quickly took an interest in doing what I could.

Unfortunately, the first place Joe suggested was a support group. Now, I know support groups do a lot of good for a lot of people facing a horde of different issues and tragedies, and I applaud them all. My experience with my one and only one support group was, however, not that kind of thing. I went for one hour, left, and never came back. The entire atmosphere in there had been at once dark, depressing, and resigned. There were fifteen other people in the room, all of them co-dependent on each other, and all hopelessly embracing a victim mentality. If I could sum up everyone's comments in one sentence it would be this: "Poor me, I'm only here because you all understand."

Maybe it was just the makeup of that particular circle of people on that particular day, but I couldn't take it. I stayed until the end of the meeting, and then when folks were talking to me one-on-one I wanted to be encouraging, and encouraged, but it was really tough. I'd just had my surgery, and I was surrounded by people whose greatest hope for the future was simply to "get by." They saw themselves as disabled. I didn't, and there was no crossing that boundary between us.

I told Joe about my experience and he agreed that maybe I'd do better in one-on-one situations. Rather than try to reassure people who were just trying to cope, maybe I could just start out as a resource for people who were weighing their options, as I had been.

That made much more sense, and even felt more comfortable. More than that, I kind of got a little inspired. I was active again, but the memories of everything I'd been through, all the questions I'd had, and all the doubts and fears were still very fresh. Unlike public speaking, I had a pretty clear idea of what I wanted to tell people in this kind of setting.

I remembered first of all that for most people considering amputation, the vast bulk of the information they have to endure is negative at best, and almost always frightening. The basic message is, "You'll probably be ambulatory, but don't expect more." And that's positioned as a best-case scenario, barring any major complications or other problems. Of course, knowing that only forced me to think about all of the possible worst-case scenarios.

The problem is the medical industry hardly ever gets to be around for the good parts. They're around during the worst moments of your life and right after they do everything they can to put you back together they have to send you home. They rarely get to witness the moments of glory that can come after.

I remembered how dark and dreary my own online research on RSD had been, and how I'd finished all that research only to be convinced I was going to spend the rest of my life in a wheelchair, drugged up or writhing in agony. Or both.

That certainly wasn't where my head was anymore. I remembered the statistic about how less than half of amputees are still active. I won't say it became my mission to change that, but I certainly did think a countervailing voice to the low expectations would serve a purpose. For me, being ambulatory was simply a baseline starting point. From there, the sky could be the limit.

Even as I was pondering that, I flashed back to my own pre-surgery mind. Before I could have ever really thought about all those things, I'd just needed to step out of the ring for a minute. I was getting pummeled with information and stories and advice and prognoses for which I had absolutely no frame of reference. Doctors were everywhere. It was overwhelming, confusing, and scary.

If there was an area where I could really be of help, I felt like it would be in just passing along the most basic information and being willing, as others had for me, to answer what had once seemed to me like the stupidest questions on earth, but questions that nonetheless had to be answered. These were the questions that physical and occupational therapists couldn't answer credibly. Thinking about life without a limb is an otherworldly concept. Only someone who's been there and done that can really offer a sense of comfort, reassurance, and meaningful advice.

Most of all, I could help demystify the whole thing. Simply by showing up I could demonstrate that I was still a regular person.

Malcolm had done that for me and I knew that just by walking into a room I might be able to do that for someone else.

Beyond addressing the fear of the unknown for others though, I did still want to try to encourage amputees and would-be amputees to plan on having an active life again.

I think that desire was fueled by personal knowledge that the more I moved around, the better I felt. At minimum, being active kept the RSD at bay, but any doctor would tell you that people who are active generally tend to feel better than those who aren't. I hoped my example could show people that the better state of being that comes with being active could, eventually, be within their reach. They could be in that percentage of amputees who were back living life to the fullest.

I'd have to get them to understand that the pain they'd have initially from the amputation, while really, really bad, was only going to be temporary. I remembered that people had tried to tell me the same thing. One guy even told me to just write the whole first year off, and focus on getting back in action in the second year. I thought that sounded pretty stupid at the time, but after a few months, I was amazed at how wise that advice became.

"That first year, your body just isn't able to do it," he'd told me. "It's been pretty well hammered—you need to let it work the trauma out of itself. Bones need to knit, bruises need to heal, and strength needs to come back. Until that's done, you only go forward in small increments."

I could tell people all about how they would come out of surgery and when the anesthesia wears off, the last thing they'd want to think about is being active again. They'd struggle just to sit up and feed themselves at first, and that was okay. All they needed to know was that for the first year, they should just go easy, and keep the bar low. They needed to let their body adjust, they needed to let themselves figure out how their prosthetic works. And they needed to manage expectations on the low end. Every day would get a little better.

I knew I had to tell them there would likely be setbacks—no point in hiding that—but I'd persuade them to ride that out and, after six months or a year, start getting on a bike again or walking around the block a few times. They'd see the value in that. With mobility and the better state of health that comes with it, there's also self-esteem, confidence, strength and, inevitably, a hunger to do more. It would mean more time doing things with family and friends. More things to look forward to, more reasons to get up every day. It would mean a better quality of life.

I committed to Joe that I'd help whenever I could. In truth, even without being as inspired as I was about what to say, there was no other answer I could give, really. You need to help someone else when you can; but for me it was more than a simple "pay it forward" kind of thing. I thought again about all that Christ had done for me, and now here I was with the tools to serve others in a very distinct and purposeful way. Saying no to that was hardly the model I wanted to show.

I started working with some of Joe's patients pretty soon after the El Cap climb, and it was through those interactions that I met some of the most amazing people. Dave Gindl was one of them.

Dave was always a fan of off-road motorcycling. He'd been out riding along a dirt road on one of his favorite after-dinner runs and, when he saw a small jump out in the middle of a field, he couldn't resist.

He knew the instant he hit the jump that he'd come up on it too fast. There was no way he was going to land on the bike, at least not in a good way, so in midair he pushed it away.

He flew for more than 30 feet, not high, but fast, and hit the ground feetfirst, like a long jumper driving into the sand. When he finally stopped and looked down at his feet, they were both pointing the wrong way.

His son, Josh, was right behind him when it happened. He saw the whole thing and called 911. The doctors were able to save both his feet but, as in my situation, it was only with a lot of spit and tape. At the time, they weren't sure he was ever going to walk again.

I first met Dave when I spoke at another men's conference. He was in his late forties, and had been living with pain and junk ankles for nearly ten years, which is a long time for a man whose job requires him to spend ten hours a day on his feet. He'd come up after my speech and given me his business card, saying he was thinking about amputating his right leg and wondered if he could talk with me.

Over the next year we met for breakfast once a month. Most of the talking was just about life in general; we actually spoke very little about him taking off his foot. He'd ask me one or two questions during the conversation, and sometimes he'd ask the same questions month after month. He was learning everything he could to make sure he would make the right decision, and I think part of that involved watching me over a period of time, to see that I was still the same person over the course of a year and not someone who just put on a happy face when he gave a speech.

As I got to know him over the months, I grew to respect him a great deal, and we became close friends. I was lucky to connect with him so early in my work with other amputees, because my conversations with him really helped shape how I talk to people. What always impressed me about him, and still does, is that he's one of those people who just oozes positive. He's always upbeat and happy in a very genuine way. He's just so in love with God and what He's done, and he's got such a powerful spirit of gratitude that I couldn't help but be drawn in. He's thankful for every day. He truly views each one as a special gift, and he can't wait to see what God has in store for him with every sunrise. I love feeling that vibe in someone's life. With trauma victims, conversations can be understandably bleak, but I found that when I met with Dave, I always walked away in a better mood than when I'd sat down, and I came to really look forward to our talks.

Ten years after his accident, at the age of forty-nine, Dave decided to go forward with the surgery. He kept his positive attitude through it all, and when we met for coffee eight months after the operation, he couldn't believe he'd waited ten years.

We're still in touch today and he's gone on to live a very rich and full life despite being short a boot. He's back riding motorcycles again and continues to have a positive outlook that is nothing less than infectious. I find that if I need a little positive boost every now and then, I'll go have coffee with Dave. He's just that kind of guy.

Along with Dave, I had the privilege of working with several trauma victims over the next several months and years. Invariably, when I spoke to a group, someone would come up to me who had a son or a brother or a friend they wanted me to talk to. I did the best I could, talking to folks on the phone if they were out of state, or visiting in person if they were nearby. I learned something from all of them. Some of the most powerful lessons, however, came from the people who were not happy to see me.

When I first heard about Mike, I had no doubt I was the right guy to talk to him. A mutual friend had heard about Mike's accident and put me in touch with Mike's brother, Randy. Like me, Mike was a climber. He'd fallen about 50 feet, hit his head and broken both of his feet. They'd taken his leg, just below the knee, in the initial surgery. He'd woken up with a limb missing, and even though I couldn't truly put myself in that kind of place, I knew that he had to accept that the leg was gone and was never coming back. I was confident I could help him make the transition to life after amputation.

When I called Randy and told him my story and who I was, he got really excited. Randy is also a climber and he was sure the common bond all three of us had would make conversation easy. He put me in touch with his parents, who I discovered were both strong believers. They asked me to come down to St. Anthony's Hospital in Lakewood, about an hour or so south. No one was sure of the full extent of Mike's injuries, particularly to his brain, but they thought talking to me could, if nothing else, lift his spirits.

Mike was still in ICU when I arrived. I couldn't find Randy or his parents anywhere, but the nurse recognized me and, since Mike was awake and talking, she let me go into his room.

He was looking away from me, toward the wall, when I walked in. I was wearing shorts, but by the time he saw me I was next to his bed and he couldn't see my legs.

"My name's Craig. I'm a climber, and I've been where you are," I said as we made eye contact and shook hands. At the word "climber" he started smiling.

"I was in an accident too," I began, as I took a couple steps back from the bed. "And I'm here to tell you—"

As his eyes drifted down and he saw my leg his whole face changed. The reaction was so visceral I couldn't even finish my sentence. Without a word, he turned his face from me and went back to looking at the wall.

I had never been shut down that hard before. I had no idea what to do and just stood there open-mouthed until the nurse, who'd watched the whole thing, told me Mike needed to rest and perhaps I should step out.

I stumbled back into the main hallway and after gazing left and right, I still couldn't find Mike's family anywhere. That was fine, because I really wanted to throw up.

As I drove home I felt like more than a failure. I felt like a complete fraud. Who the heck did I think I was, presuming I could just walk into anybody's room and tell them I knew how they felt, and that everything was going to be just fine? What if I'd just done Mike more harm than good? What business did I have passing myself off like this? I was no licensed therapist. I was no certified counselor. I was just a guy who, it turns out, didn't know as much about helping other people as he thought he did.

It ate me up all weekend until I realized, once again, that what I really needed to do was shut up. It wasn't my place to tell anybody how to deal with something. More often than not it was the trauma victim's family, not the trauma victim, that asked me to visit. I'd been taking that on as my mission to go in and help the person solve their problem. That, I suddenly realized, was not my job.

And that was hard to take. Many men, and I'm one of them, have it in their blood to be problem solvers. And that drives many women crazy when all they really want a man to do is listen. This was no different. In my own experience in the hospital, there was no way someone was going to come in and tell me what decisions to make and to just buck up. The future *me* could have come into that hospital and told me he understood how I felt, and I still wouldn't have accepted it. The suffering we all endure in life is one thing that, no matter what reality is, we perceive as something uniquely our own.

> **The suffering we all endure in life is one thing that, no matter what reality is, we perceive as something uniquely our own.**

I don't know why I didn't think of that before I started all of this, especially considering I'd made a vow after that phone call the night before my surgery to never offer an opinion unless I was asked. People didn't need me to fix things. They just needed me to listen and, at the right times with the right attitude, offer encouragement and guidance. Beyond that, they needed to own their situation on their own terms—because that's about the only thing in their control at that point.

I realized I could serve them best simply by falling silent and letting them process things themselves as they spoke. If my presence there was something of a comfort, and if, by the time I left the room, they felt a little more empowered to figure out their pain and their recovery, then that would be a success.

The following Monday the phone rang. It was Mike's dad, calling to ask if I'd had the chance to stop by Mike's room. I told him everything that had happened, and how terrible I felt. His father assured me it was okay. They now knew a little more about Mike's injuries.

"Mike doesn't even remember you coming to visit," his father told me. "His head injury was pretty serious. He's got some brain damage, and for the moment, he's not keeping any short-term memories."

Relieved as I was that I hadn't made Mike's recovery worse, I was sorry to hear the news about his condition, and told his father so.

"We don't know how this is going to turn out," his dad said. "We might not know for months."

I told him I'd keep them all in my prayers, and we hung up.

The epilogue to Mike's story, just like real life, is bittersweet. His brain injury was indeed pretty serious, but as I stayed in touch with his family, Randy and I became friends, and I eventually began talking with Mike again. Today I still get text messages from Mike saying he's praying or thinking about me. He never misses an opportunity to just cheer me on. And, as his father told me, he never remembered my first visit. I, however, never forgot it.

Since those early days, I've worked closely with dozens of people and done "drive-by" counseling with dozens more. I've also started to work with some of the injured vets coming back from Iraq, many of whom have lost limbs, where we all go climbing for the day as part of the process of getting them reacclimated to the world over here. I can't imagine what it's like to switch from an environment where your life is at risk 24-7, and where your job is to kill people and blow things up, and then come back

here where that sort of thing is, shall we say, frowned upon. Climbing together, especially with strangers, helps teach things like trust and good communication—tools they need as they transition to a safe, low-key environment. For me, it's been a really cool way to meet some of the men and women serving our country and, to their credit, the vets I've worked with so far have all had the most remarkable attitudes. Collectively, they've preserved that adventurous spirit that was surely part of their decision to join the military in the first place, and there's a prevalent mood of "I want to overcome this thing that has happened to me." As we climb together, it's nothing but smiles with this crowd. They inspire me, and I get to experience a unique joy in opening their eyes to the kind of rich and full life they can still have.

As for how I start working with someone nowadays, either Joe will call me or—something that actually happens quite a lot—people will seek me out. They'll hear my story and file it away, and then something happens to someone they know and they remember me. I don't make flyers and I'm not in the phone book, but I can easily be found.

Today when I go into a hospital room it's much different than it was that time with Mike. My mistakes in visiting him were by no means my last, but I continued to learn lessons. Even now with each visit I'm hopefully getting better at helping people come to terms with and sort through their own situations. I've seen how empowering it is when people feel like they understand, through the presence of a living, breathing person standing in front of them, a little more about what could be happening with them. It takes some of the mystery away and with it, some of the fear of the unknown. That fear gets replaced by confidence, and even by a sense of peace. It's amazing to witness.

Selfish as it sounds, I also feel like I'm getting something out of visiting others. I can be in the middle of a high pain day, feeling like crap, and upon stepping into the orthopedic ward I'll suddenly remember how far I've come. I'll remember that I'm visiting people at the very beginning of what will be a very long process, who are still hurting, still scared, and still confused. I'll see them all busted up, bloody, medicated, and I'll forget about whatever was going on with me. I know at the end of every visit I'm going to get up, walk out, go home and hug my wife, but simple things like that are months away for the person in front of me. It helps me keep my own problems in perspective and remember why I'm there in the first place.

Joe encouraged me to continue speaking to folks as just another regular guy, and I make a point not to speak about what I've achieved climbing. I just tell them I'm a climber. From there I give opinions only when asked, and do my best to tell people what they can expect if, as they weigh the options of amputation, they decide to go down that road. I start by telling the story of my own accident. It helps put everything else I have to say into the right perspective.

I don't promise anyone they'll be able to do the things I've done; I just let my story paint the picture of my accident, how bad off I was, and how I was in a situation similar to where they are right at that moment. From there, I just let my body tell the rest. They can see where my bar is, and they can set theirs wherever they want. I let them know I'll be one of the people going through this with them, if they want, every step of the way. I give them my cell number, which, admittedly, creates room for a lot of interruptions, but I view that as part of serving.

I remember counseling one woman in particular, Joan. I only actually met her once, but before that we talked on the phone more than a dozen times over a few weeks. She had hit a tree while skiing and badly injured her leg. She was a hairstylist by profession, and after years of standing on her feet for eight-hour days, only to end up crumpled in a chair in misery every evening, she was giving serious thought to amputation. She'd call me at random times with all kinds of random questions, as I'd encouraged her to do, until she ultimately decided to go through with the surgery. She'd made her appointment, but the big day hadn't arrived yet, and she called to talk about an issue I could identify with only too well.

"Craig, my leg doesn't hurt as bad anymore," she said. "It feels like it's getting better, and I'm wondering if maybe I should hold off."

I'm always careful to avoid telling people what to do. I'm not their doctor, I don't walk around in their skin, and only they really know what's best for them. The best I could do, knowing how similar her situation was to mine, was tell her what I'd thought in those same doubt-laden moments.

"For me, it kept coming back to the fact that my ankle was junk," I told her. "Even if it didn't hurt, I still couldn't do anything with it. I had to remember that as good as the good days were, they were outnumbered by bad days, and sometimes the bad was really, really bad.

I had to ask myself if this was really the life I was going to be happy with, or was I willing to try for something better."

She ended up going ahead with the surgery, and is moving on with her life quite well. She told me later that it gave her a good perspective once we finally met to see me get around and be so open and upbeat about what had happened to me.

Other folks I talk to are so gung ho that I feel compelled to rein them in a little. I can usually tell in the first couple minutes whether someone has an attitude that's going to get them back into their old life or not. Don't get me wrong, it's never easy on anyone, but there is an unmistakable group of people who just want to get up, get out of the hospital, and get on with their lives. It's hard, but I have to tell those folks to put the brakes on and let their bodies heal before they ask it to keep up with their minds.

More often than not, my first visits lead into conversations that might last more than an hour that day, or might be ongoing for weeks and months. At the very least, they trigger a series of questions, all the same questions I'd asked when I was in their place. At first I tried to get into the minutiae of healing, but I quickly realized (and remembered) that no one in that situation cares about the minor details. They just want the big picture. Before anyone wanted to talk about the mechanics of playing tennis again, they needed to back up the train and get answers to questions much more fundamental. How are they going to hug their wives, tie their shoes, or make a sandwich or, like me, get to the bathroom in the middle of the night? There were also the deeper questions, about how friends might treat them, what they'd actually look like, and whether or not their spouses would still find them attractive. And the big question, could amputation end up being a huge mistake that could never be corrected?

The biggest question I get is, why would you willingly cut your leg off? I give them the same answer I gave to that small group of men I spoke to right before my surgery. As I've said, it's impossible to tell my story without talking about what God has done for me. I find it's remarkably easy to present that as just part of the facts of my story, leading up to the conclusion that, through a series of unfortunate events I actually became the person I really wanted to be. I'm not shy about telling them how smoothly it went once I realized I couldn't fix this by myself, or how things changed once I let God be in control.

Nor am I shy about suggesting that they be open to what God is going to show them.

What I've noticed though, in telling that story, is that people who've experienced the kind of trauma and loss that I have either run to God or run away from God. There's never any middle ground, and I've always been puzzled by that. For some it comes down to disappointment with God, and, unfortunately, they leave it at that. Others realize, as Philip Yancey pointed out in his book *Disappointment with God*, the only other alternative is disappointment *without* God.

> **What I've noticed is that people who've experienced the kind of trauma and loss that I have either run to God or run away from God. There's never any middle ground.**

I can only hope, as I sit down with someone for the first time, that they'll keep their heart open. I know in the end it isn't up to me. I just need to keep stepping out in faith, and letting God do the rest.

12

MOVING ON

God's plan is hardly ever our plan.

When I think about where I am today, I can tell you quite sincerely that this is not the life I would have chosen. I made no plans to crush almost everything in my body that matters, wave and smile at death, and then go out and speak to crowds about what happened. Nor would I have chosen the costs that have come with it—my day-to-day life with pain is hardly sunshine and lollipops, but God laid this life out for me and gave me the strength to pick it up and run with it. Now that I can finally see where it's going, I wouldn't change anything about it.

You could say my story is one of hope and one with a happy ending, but it's not over by any means. Nor is it the classic, storybook happy ending. In our real world, even happy endings have strings attached.

You'd think someone who has directly seen God work would constantly put God first in every aspect of his life. You'd think someone who's seen God perform real miracles would be above getting angry in traffic. Or being self-centered. Or letting anything get in the way of his faith.

I'm not.

I used to marvel at the story of how the Jews, as they were being led out of Egypt, would forget about who God was and what He'd done for them. I mean, for crying out loud, He parted the Red Sea for them. He fed them manna from heaven. God's presence was a visible pillar of fire in front of them every day and night, yet they still forgot Him and His promises over and over again.

I don't marvel at that anymore. I've seen in my own experience how quickly old habits and ways of thinking come back. I've seen over and over how I get so absorbed in my own problems and needs and wants that God becomes an accessory again.

The scary part is it's not a conscious decision to lapse into old patterns. Unless I decide *not* to let that happen, it just does. I try to do my best, but even remembering all the amazing things God has done in my life doesn't suddenly take all my problems away. Stuff comes up and distracts me, and shows me constantly that my faith, despite everything, is still as fragile as anyone else's.

> **Stuff comes up and distracts me, and shows me constantly that my faith, despite everything, is still as fragile as anyone else's.**

There are times I'm certain God is working, and other times I feel like He's completely left the building. It's hard to admit that, because even I think, as most people who meet me do, that my faith should be rock solid. It's frustrating to have days or weeks where I feel lost and alone and shattered. God just seems so silent. But it's just like that old "Footprints" poem affixed to the front of millions of refrigerators around the world. In the times I thought God was being most silent, when I thought I was most alone, that's when He was carrying me through.

That sounds like a simple thing to remember, but I still forget, even now. No one should think for one minute that I get up every day and have this incredibly close relationship with God, where He's constantly in the forefront of my thoughts. I try to be sensitive and look for His guidance, but the truth is, some days I do a pretty good job of following Him, some days I'm mediocre at it, and a lot of days I'm really bad at it. Often, that's because of the pain. There's no escape from it, and it's the biggest reminder of what I said about happy endings coming with strings attached.

Long gone are the days in the hospital where I could take some heavy drugs and pour myself into sweet oblivion for eight or nine hours. Instead I sleep for about two hours before muscle stiffness or some other pain yanks me out of sleep and I have to readjust my body. Every night is the same. I can only sleep on my side or my back. I used to sleep on my stomach. It was always the most comfortable for me. Now when I try, it's like trying to bend with a board attached to my spine, screwed into my lower back and neck. The same fused vertebrae that help me walk upright make it impossible to lie prone comfortably.

Every morning I'm pulled from the small amount of sleep I get by the pain in my back and neck. My hands are usually numb and hurt, but the pain in my back from lying down all night is what wrenches my eyes open. It won't leave me alone until I'm upright and moving. All my muscles are inflamed, stiff and tight, and I usually have a headache. When my neck healed at C6, it didn't align itself correctly with C5, leaving me with chronic pain, nerve damage, and pinched nerves that send stabbing pins and needles down the right side of my body. Inevitably it drives me into a sitting position, which feels like pulling myself out of wet cement. It's painful, but it's better than laying still. I have to roll on my side and push up with my arms, and once I'm finally sitting up, I have to hang there for a minute or two to steel myself for what comes next.

I keep the leg next to the bed, and after I either walk or crawl to the bathroom, I have to make my way upstairs to the kitchen. Unless I have an RSD flare-up, that walk up the stairs is the hardest part of my day, because nothing is working right yet. I still have to look down to make sure my foot is actually touching the floor. Everything I broke ten years ago hurts. It's even worse if there's a storm coming. I feel it in my joints about a day in advance, as the barometric pressure changes, and it feels like my whole body is being squeezed. By the time I finally make it to the kitchen, I'm the human equivalent of a condemned wharf building.

The first thing I do is slam down a four-pill cocktail of drugs—the first of three doses of meds I take every day—to stay ahead of the RSD, regulate my bladder and the muscles in my abdomen, and knock down the swelling.

I used to get hung up on taking so many drugs, fearful of what having so many chemicals in my system would do to me. For a time at the beginning of it all, I even tried to wean myself off them. That did not end well.

After ten years I've adopted a "You know what? It's fine" attitude about it. I don't mind carrying pill bottles with me everywhere I go. I'm taking controlled doses on a doctor's orders that, as a result of the accident, my body cannot function properly without. I still don't like it, but I might as well not like water or air either if I'm going to get hung up on what my body needs to work right.

Once the pills are down, I drink a bunch of coffee. It's a little known secret in the medical world that coffee actually gets the pills to dissolve and work faster. It's not just in my head, I really do notice a difference if I chug down coffee with my meds.

With the drugs and java in my gut, I just sit for about thirty minutes and let everything work. That time makes the slog upstairs worth it. Our house faces due east and with a clear view of the eastern horizon I watch the sun rise every day. There are some mornings I simply can't take my eyes off it.

When the kids were younger I'd also use that quiet time for devotionals and prayer. Now that Mayah is older and going to school earlier, she's awake with me and we get to spend that time together. I'm so thankful for that. She's getting to an age where fathers and daughters can easily drift apart. I'll gladly walk up those stairs every day for the rest of my life just to have that time with her.

As the meds take the edge off, I can feel the muscles loosening and I start to feel better. As the day goes on, the pain usually becomes white noise in the background. It never goes away completely, unless I can find my way into a hot tub. Whether it's one minute or one hour, just being able to float in that warm, soothing water makes the pain dissipate all the way, only to come back bitter and angry when I surrender to gravity again.

On "good days" the pain doesn't get above a 2 or a 3 on the scale and I can manage to ignore it. On a bad day it can get up to a 5 or 6, and I'll feel like I've been hit by a small imported car. But even then while I'm more aware of it, it doesn't completely shut me down. The only thing that does that is the RSD. That's the pain that stops me cold.

It'll come out of nowhere. There's no predicting or anticipating it, and once it's there it's like the Terminator. It can't be bargained with. It can't be reasoned with. It doesn't feel pity, or remorse, or fear. And it absolutely will not stop.

I might go three or four weeks with nothing and then it will hit. A switch flips on and the pain level instantly goes up to a 10 and keeps drilling. It's like an electrical current from the lowest part of my stump all the way up to my hip. It's a hard surge for a few seconds, then it shuts off for ten, then surges on again for two, then off for ten, and the pattern repeats over and over. Imagine someone hitting your hand with a hammer as hard as they can, then waiting ten seconds and doing it again.

It becomes a form of mental torture as much as a source of physical agony—I'm constantly gritting my teeth and waiting for the next surge. It might last an hour, or it might last a day. Sometimes it can go on for half a week. Sleeping is impossible. Functioning is impossible. I just have to keep gobbling Nuerontin until it catches up and shuts the gate in that nerve.

On those days, it doesn't matter what I had planned, or what I'd hoped to accomplish. I'll be down for the count. Between the pain and the fogged out feeling that comes with upping the pain meds, I'm just done for that day.

I've never been much of a yeller, and so far the RSD hasn't changed that, but I'd be lying if I said I wasn't hissing through my teeth pretty good when it comes on. And when it finally ends, the only thing I know for sure is that it will be back, at least once, in the next month.

With pain you learn a lot.

With pain you learn a lot. You learn that you have no control of your life, especially when it can come out of nowhere and shut you down almost instantly. My body gets so tired from it that by late afternoon I start getting short-tempered and I know it's a good time for me to go off by myself. It's easy to lapse into self-centered ways of thinking, and acting, but as I start to get caught up in that, and as my focus on God falters, it's actually the pain itself that snaps me back. And because of that, strange as it sounds, I've learned that when the pain is at its height it's a good time to connect with God.

When the RSD explodes, I know I'm not going anywhere or doing anything, so it's a good time to pray. I can't really read the Bible in those moments—it's too hard to focus on reading as the pain kicks my body and the drugs do their thing, so I just sit and talk with God. I ask questions. I tell Him what's bothering me. I look for answers and nuances I may have missed as I've been speeding through life along with everyone else. The pain forces me to slow down, to be present, and to focus on the important things.

For that reason I don't ask God to take the pain away anymore, like I did in the hospital when everything I thought I'd known about pain got thrown out the window. That said, I'm not above asking Him to maybe make it a little less, but I never forget that for me, the alternative to having that pain is not being here at all. Or being paralyzed, having brain damage, or being so drugged up that I can't have any kind of meaningful relationship with my wife, my kids, or any of the people closest to me.

With that focus I tell Him what's on my mind, then I just shut up and listen. God doesn't speak to me in some booming voice or anything, but if I lie there and listen long enough, as the thoughts rush through my head, I try to filter out the ones that I've put there and let God's soft whisper rise to the surface. It's not easy, but if I'm still and silent long enough I can almost always see a way through whatever problems I'm facing, and I realize that none of them are too large or too hard, and that I never need to deal with any of them on my own.

> God doesn't speak to me in some booming voice or anything, but if I lie there and listen long enough, as the thoughts rush through my head, I try to filter out the ones that I've put there and let God's soft whisper rise to the surface.

People who don't know that part of my story think it's pretty crazy that I find the pain, in some ways, a little refreshing. Or maybe that's not the right word, but rather than dread a pain flare-up, I kind of welcome it because I know it will leave me in a good place when it's over. That has really helped my attitude in dealing with my pain. And my prognosis.

With age, my joints will become stiffer, and I've already been described as someone who will be the most arthritic man in Colorado sometime in the next twenty years. I don't think it's going to get much worse than it is today. Maybe I'm being naïve, but I talk to people with chronic arthritis and as I hear them tell me what they're going through, empathetic as I am, I realize I'm well past that already.

The RSD is going to get worse; that's probably inevitable. As I get older, I'm going to slow down. I won't be able to keep those nerves firing at a constant pace, so it's going to get the opening it's waiting for and it's going to spread. It's at my hip now, but it's taken nine years to get there. It's going to spread, but hopefully it'll be a slow spread, and won't ever confine me to a wheelchair.

Every time my doctors look at an x-ray, they talk about more surgeries. They think they should fuse my neck at C5 and C6, which would relieve some of the pressure on my right side. They think they should fuse my left ankle, which they still describe as "chewed up" and being held together by a couple of screws. But the cost of those "fixes" is just too much. Fusing my ankle would just put more hardware in me that I don't want, and effectively remove my ankle joint, eliminating what little flexibility I have below my knees. In my neck, I already have trouble moving my head from side to side, which makes doing what I do hard enough. Fusing those bones could make it impossible, and there's no guarantee that either surgery would solve any of my chronic pain problems. Unlike the decision to cut off my leg, my best hope for a good quality of life today is to leave those parts of me just as they are, flawed and weak, but functional and doing the best they can. Just like the rest of me.

Chuck Swindoll once said, "We cannot change the inevitable. The only thing we can do is play on the one string we have, and that is our attitude. I am convinced that life is 10 percent what happens to me, and 90 percent how I react to it. And so it is with you . . . we are in charge of our attitudes."

I use that as the signature in all of my emails. I get to make the choice to have a good attitude on a daily basis, and sometimes on a minute-by-minute basis, about how my body feels, and what lies ahead. To me, the message there is, choose a good outcome and it will happen. It may not be the one I thought should happen, but it will be a good one God has made happen. It will be one that will benefit me and the people around me.

The point is, I don't really know what my life will be like in twenty more years, but there's little I can do about it either way, so there's no reason to obsess about it. My bedrock is knowing God has a plan; that's what I go back to. It may not be what I want or think it should be, but I can choose to have a positive attitude about it or not. I could fight it every day, or I can realize that God's plan is better than mine, and move forward.

Often, that's easier said than done. I know He has plans for me and they are meant to help and grow me, but I admit sometimes I get so self-focused that I forget that something I might do or say can affect someone in a positive or negative way.

God almost never works the way I think He will. I never know whose life He's touching through me. I do things in climbing that I may not think are a big deal, but it might mean something in someone else's life that's bigger and more significant than I could have imagined. They're seeing God act in my life and they're seeing that God can act in their life too. God sees the big picture; I just see the small screen. Every day is another square in the tapestry of what God's plan looks like, and maybe if I'm lucky one day I'll get to see it all.

I probably get the chance to tell my story a couple times a week, even now. Thousands of people have heard the story of how God is working in my life because of my prosthetic leg. People will be very emotional and sorry that I lost my leg. Or they ask if God is so good or my faith is so strong then why wasn't I healed. I tell them all the same thing. Because I lost my leg, I was able to do what I love. Because God didn't heal me, even though He could have, I get to tell the story of how He took a terrible accident and turned it into this really cool life.

To this day I wear shorts as often as I can. I want people to see my leg. I want them to be curious and ask what happened. I want them to ask me how I've managed to overcome so much and accomplish so much, so I can tell them I can only do it because God is so amazing. As unsteady as I am in my day-to-day walk, nothing gets me back in balance like telling the story of what God has done for me. For a guy who never wanted to talk about his faith, I can hardly wait for the next opportunity.

> **As unsteady as I am in my day-to-day walk, nothing gets me back in balance like telling the story of what God has done for me.**

That's why I would not go back in time and prevent the accident if I could. It wasn't a fun experience and I certainly wouldn't run out and do it again, but life after the fall has been a pretty good trade-off. All the incredible things that have happened have stemmed from that experience. The convenient parking isn't so bad either . . .

I'm sure without the accident I'd have gone on to live a fine life, but I'd have continued to compartmentalize God for the rest of it. I might have never known what it means to step out in faith. I might never have learned that when I take one step toward God, even if it goes against every grain of what I think I want, He takes ninety-nine steps toward me.

The fall was a catalyst that turned me into who I am today. My accident led me not just to the life I thought I wanted, but to the life I now see God had in mind for me. God got my attention. And I rejoice for it.

EPILOGUE

THE LIST

This list started as nothing more than an idle thought.

I was sitting at home a few months after having my leg amputated and I was bored out of my mind. A man can only do so many wheelies in his wheelchair before he has to find something else.

The warmer weather was also making me a little antsy. Ever since I first started climbing, the onset of spring would fill me with a raw, leg-twitching energy. Warm weather meant the real climbing season was coming. It meant being outdoors, having new adventures, and saying goodbye to cold gray days of staring at the walls. With the first day of spring, I was like a bear ready to come out of hibernation.

That year was no exception, but only a few months out of surgery, climbing was still a big question mark. I didn't know if my body would be physically capable of it, and all the doctors had to say was "no way." I wasn't ready to believe I could be climbing again soon, nor was I willing to accept that I wouldn't.

I had to do something to ease my climbing withdrawal, so I started thinking about what I would do if I really was going to climb again. What climbs would I do first? Which ones would really memorialize my ascension to being a climber once again?

I had always focused on being a strong, well-rounded climber, solid and capable in all the disciplines: trad, ice, bouldering, walls. Surfers have a name for a guy who's solid, trusted, and capable in any situation. They call him a waterman. Climbers have a similar term: hardman. It's a name that says this guy can handle anything. Earn that moniker, and people will always know you're a climber.

I'd been in that zone before. I'd done it all and I'd put a lot of really solid climbs under my belt. If only I could do that again . . .

As I sat there in the middle of my kitchen, I realized that if I could repeat some of those climbs of the past, maybe even get a First Disabled Ascent on them, I could one day say I'd completed the journey around this circle. It would really mean I was whole again.

I started to get serious about the idea and putting pen to paper. I knew I couldn't just pick random climbs. I had to focus on climbs that made sense for a guy with a prosthetic foot—even though Cyndy says using it is completely "aid climbing," which she says is cheating.

I also wanted to pick routes that had meant something to me. It didn't matter if they were really difficult or really easy, all that mattered was that in some way they had resonated with my soul. They had made me feel free and alive.

It didn't take long. In fact the hardest part was narrowing the list down, but when I was done, I had a list of six climbs. Over the years, the list would evolve and more climbs would find their way onto it, but that initial list became my inspiration. I didn't pursue it to try to stop global warming, or to end hunger, or even to bring about world peace. That list was just for me. And as I formed it, I had no idea how deeply meaningful the experience of finishing each climb would be. That was the true gift and joy of The List. At the finish of every climb, I could look back and be astonished at what a different person I'd become—in every imaginable way—since I'd first done each climb. I had no idea of the amazing richness that perspective would add to my life.

#1 The Diagonal—Summer 2005

This one was a no-brainer for a spot on The List. It's the climb that resonates the most with me because it's a climb Cyndy and I did together on one of our first dates.

I'd first met Cyndy when we were both in Pennsylvania. She lived in Colorado at the time and knew I was planning to move out there, so she told me to give her a call when I got to town.

With an invitation like that, I couldn't get to Colorado fast enough.

When I called her and we talked about going climbing, she told me about a place called Combat Rock, a big granite dome right above a town called Loveland. How fitting. She told me about a classic climb there called The Diagonal. It's not a really challenging climb, it's only rated a 5.9, but it's a real nice, accessible climb and, I discovered, a good way to spend a quality afternoon with someone. We made plans to give it a try and drove out together.

From the parking area, it's about a mile walk along a trail that drops you down into a valley and then takes you up a steep hill to the base of the climb. We had a nice talk on the way there, but I hadn't climbed much in Colorado and my thoughts kept coming back to really wanting to impress her. I needed to be at my confident, capable, climbing best.

The climb itself is a long, diagonal crack that runs up for a full pitch, about 100 feet, then goes on up into a roof system—a large cap of rock with a perfect crack that runs to the right and gives the climber a path to overcome the roof. The movement along it is really cool—you're always leaning to the left on the first pitch. As a traditional climb, it's one where your whole body is out of the crack except for your fingertips. It needs gear and takes gear really well, everywhere except "the crux," which is the name given to the hardest part of any climb. In this particular crux, the crack pinches down until it's impossible to even cram your fingertips in it, and you have to power up through a short section of blank rock until the crack opens up again.

When Cyndy and I went back to climb it again after the surgery, I knew it was well within my ability, but I also knew it was a climb that put a lot of dependence on my feet. The power moves at the crux were easily done with two feet, but I wasn't sure what it'd be like with only one.

I wasn't as concerned with impressing Cyndy this time though, which was good because suffice it to say my original plan for doing the route didn't exactly work. The plan basically relied on sticking my prosthetic foot into a parallel crack that ran along with the main route and fishing around with my other foot for little nubbins on the granite. It worked well until about halfway up, when the lower crack got so small that I couldn't get the titanium foot into it anymore.

I wasn't anywhere near tired, but without being able to put weight on one of my feet anymore, I suddenly had a pretty big puzzle to solve. I was only hanging on by my fingers, and that wasn't going to last too long.

I put a solid piece in place and tried to think. The only solution that presented itself was to finish the climb just like any able-bodied climber would—with both feet on the rock face. That was a touch

ironic, since I'd come up with the whole "foot-in-the-crack plan" precisely because I didn't think I could smear the foot on the rock face
and expect it to hold. Now that plan A had failed, I just had to give it
a try and hope the foot would stick—I really didn't need it to go slipping off, smashing my knees and face into the rock.

I gave it a test and found, to my joy, that it worked just fine. I made
it all the way up to the first belay point without a problem, and I felt
really, really good. In control. I could do this.

The second pitch was a little tricky too, and I'm sure my ascent
was not a pretty one—certainly not the kind that would have earned
me another date with Cyndy back in the day—but I made it. Cyndy
joined me at the top after a few minutes and we just took a little time
to savor the moment. Against all the odds, we'd made it back to this
spot together. The whole climb had taken maybe an hour, but it created a memory that would last forever. Again.

#2 Piano Traverse—Summer and Fall 2007

Climbing may define me as a person, but bouldering is what defines
me as a climber. It has always been my favorite discipline of the sport.
Some people like to go out for a couple hours of jogging or cycling. As
for me, I always went bouldering.

There is a world-class bouldering area near Fort Collins called
Horsetooth Reservoir. It's one of those incredibly picturesque Colorado places. There's lots of water and pine trees ringed with huge
sandstone cliffs. You could climb there all your life and not even come
close to doing all the bouldering problems it offers—there are thousands of them up there. In short, it was my playground.

It's also home to Piano Traverse. There's a huge boulder, about 15
feet tall and almost perfectly round, and the traverse is a crack that
runs from one end of it all the way around to the other side. The whole
thing also leans over slightly, so it's extremely "foot intensive"; I couldn't
try to fake my way through the footwork with my prosthetic. It's the
kind of climbing that forces you to climb smart, and it was always one
of my favorite practice spots. I knew it would be a good one to work on
to recalibrate my new body for climbing, and once I was finally strong
enough after the surgery it was one of the first places I went.

I felt horrible as I slotted my fingers into the starting holds and
made my first go of it. I was weak and over-gripping everything

instead of doing what I knew I should, which was relying on my skeleton. For a climber, to rely on your muscles is to fail quickly. A smart climber uses his skeleton to hang on and the muscles just move you along. I was shocked at how difficult it was. In the past, it had been nothing. Back when I had two feet I practically had every move memorized and could simply power through it. Not anymore. My body couldn't move on it the way it used to. Back in the day I'd have gone out there and bouldered around for a couple hours before heading home. Now, after only half an hour, I was worn out from my fingers on down. It was a complete slap-in-the-face reality check. I couldn't deny it anymore. I was a disabled climber.

But that didn't mean I had to lie down and accept that I just couldn't do this. I went back to Piano over and over again for weeks, trying to figure out how to make my body work on it. I'd see minor improvement here and there, but there was always a spot that frustrated me. It was a corner point on the boulder right near the end of the traverse. I'd always get to that point and, in trying to round it, fall off. I must have tried it a dozen times, knowing that if I could just get around that stupid corner I'd have it dialed.

The whole process was a phenomenal experience in learning how my new body worked. Every time I tried, the Piano helped me relearn a little bit more about climbing smart and, with this body, climbing smarter than I ever had before. That was the climb that first inspired me to try sanding my prosthetic foot down, and later, to try gluing climbing rubber to it.

It was also the climb that taught me how much more cautious I needed to be. Eventually I made it around that corner, and when I returned with a friend a week later to show off, he asked me if I wanted to lay down a pad at the corner. There's a sharp rock there, and if you slip off at the corner, you can end up landing on it and getting hurt unless you lay down a pad. I told him no. I was feeling confident.

Of course, my hand and foot slipped at the critical point and off I went. I missed the sharp rock on the way down, but I flatbacked, hard, onto another rock. No one was more surprised than me when I stood right up. I knew exactly how much worse that could have been, and I just shook my head. That would have been a really stupid way to get hurt, perhaps permanently. After that I never overlooked a safety option again.

#3 Winchester Pumped—Summer 2008

Winchester Pumped in Wyoming is another climb I'd done with Cyndy early in our relationship. It's in the middle of a beautiful lime-stone climbing area called Wild Iris where aspen groves grow right up to the base of the rocks, and cliffs seem to shoot straight out of the forest floor. What also made this climb special was it was the most difficult climb (5.11) I'd ever "on-sighted," meaning I climbed it the first time I saw it without any practice, research, or planning, and without watching anyone else climb it first. No equipment was placed in advance either. I'd had to navigate and think and problem-solve my way up the rock, figuring out the route by sight, feel, and gut, all extemporaneously.

Six years after the accident, I walked to the base of Winchester again, ready to take it on one more time. By that point I had been climbing a lot. I felt good.

It's a relatively short climb, about half a pitch (around 80 feet or so) and, despite its rating, it's a pretty straightforward climb for the first 60 feet. It gets more technical from there until you're literally clipping the last bolt and it's only five feet to the anchor. The holds get much smaller there, and covering that last section takes a lot of sustained aggressive moves, pulling on small "crimpers."

Needless to say, I was a little surprised on that return climb when I suddenly found myself near the anchor. The climb had gone quickly, but at the anchor I was barely hanging on. I'd climbed too fast, per-haps a little scared, and gripped too hard. Trying to get to the anchor from where I was wasn't going to work. I worked left and found some small positive holds that led me to the anchor, and the finish of the climb. The problem was it felt like I barely made it, like I wasn't totally in control on the climb. I wanted to try again, and be as smooth as I could.

I went down, took a little rest and had a little food before I started up again. Once again I made it to the hard section pretty smoothly. I'd trended to the left on the last attempt, so I thought maybe I had read things wrong and this time I tried to trend to the right. I gripped on to a chunk of limestone and as I started to pull up on it, right when I needed that hold most, the whole thing came off in my hand and I was falling.

It was a complete surprise fall, which is actually the best kind because it's over before you know what happened. There's none of that nauseating fear of falling right before it happens—you just blink and you're dangling.

It was also a very short fall, only a few feet, but that was enough excitement for me. I lowered to the ground and told Cyndy, "You know what? I'm good with this one."

#4 Punk Rock Traverse—June 2011

Punk Rock Traverse was another favorite bouldering puzzle in Horse-tooth Reservoir. Back when I'd had two feet I had it so dialed in that I could do it in tennis shoes.

Like Piano Traverse, it was a humbling and humiliating experience to return. Even before the crux there's a point that requires doing two moves together (a mini-crux) and my body just couldn't handle the choreography needed to pull it off. I used to be able to just hook my foot into a little crack and work my way around, but when I tried it with my prosthetic, the stupid thing actually got stuck.

I fell off over and over. For three months I kept coming back for more. I tried different moves and different strategies. I tried working on it in sections. All the information about the climb that I used to rely on to complete it was gone. More than once, I gave serious thought to taking this one off The List. It was just a stupid traverse anyway.

But I kept at it and by mid-spring I had almost made it all the way to the end. I'd figured out how to bypass the mini-crux, but the very end is just as tricky and I hadn't yet made it through when we decided to go up there one day with friends. I remember how unbelievably hot it was that day—around 95 degrees.

One of my friends wanted me to show some basics on how to work Punk Rock, so I chalked up and started around. I honestly didn't feel very good in my climbing that day. I was working it too hard, but before I knew it I was at the end. I'd finished. It was one of those weird quirky things where my body just got it done. My friends were a little curious about why I was so excited, so I took a little joy in telling them what a frustrating experience the last three months on that rock had been.

I came back to Punk Rock in 2011 with a film crew. I'd been selected as one of the athletes to be profiled on a show called *The Season* that year. I thought for sure there'd be no problem. I fell off seven times. On camera. And when I finally got it right, we had to call it a wrap for the day since I tore up my fingers so bad on it.

#5 The Pear—June 2007

On Lumpy Ridge in Estes Park, there's something called The Book. It's a ginormous, 1,000-foot-tall cliff and there's a climbing route on it called The Pear. For the life of me, I have no idea why. There's nothing pear-like about it. Even so, it was one of the first climbs to earn a permanent place on The List.

Cyndy had introduced me to it not too long after I moved to Colorado, saying it was one of those climbs I just had to do. I was still something of an east coast face climber at the time and was only just beginning to learn the "crack climbing style." Climbing The Pear is what made me fall in love with crack climbing. It's an easy 5.8 climb, and it's so comfortable that you can't help but enjoy it. I call it the Idiot's Guide to Crack Climbing.

It's six pitches to the top, and once you get there you're rewarded with an incredible view of the whole Estes Valley. I remember standing there that first time with Cyndy, both of us falling in love, and looking at that view.

I returned to The Pear in 2007 but, much as I enjoyed the good memories there, the thing that was most on my mind as we got out of the car was the two-mile hike in. I was getting around fine by then, but that's still a long way to go on a prosthetic. And the last quarter mile is nothing but steep switchbacks. It feels like you're going straight uphill. I remembered it was a slog even with two feet.

The hike went quickly enough and it turned out to be a really great day. The climb itself went flawlessly, but it was another special moment of appreciating how much things had changed since I'd first climbed that route, and what a different person I'd become. Back then Cyndy had been a girl I was dating. Now it was the same valley, but the woman I was with had become my wife and mother to our kids. Many things had changed, but she was still my best friend.

#6 Yosemite, Serenity Crack—June 2011

I hadn't expected to do El Capitan again as soon as I did, but it's only one of several Yosemite climbs that had fed my passion for the sport. Serenity Crack, in the Royal Arches area, was another.

When I was with Hans on the first El Cap trip, I was just focused on making that climb. I didn't even look at the others. Later, after we finished El Cap, other climbs weren't even an option. I was so blown out after that climb that I just called it good and went home. I was excited about being the first amputee to climb El Cap in a day, but my body felt broken.

The next year we went back to Yosemite as a family and, while Cyndy's mom watched the kids, Cyndy and I went to take a look at Serenity. It's a neat climb; I'd done it back in 1992 and I remembered it being a lot of fun. The whole first pitch is pin scars for 30 feet or so. It's like gripping a bowling ball until, after that initial stretch, the crack opens up and you can start putting in gear.

The climb starts out as a 5.10, but gets moderately more difficult the higher you get. Once you reach the crack you can motor up to the end of the first pitch pretty quickly. For the second pitch you work your way up the left side of twin cracks, but as they go higher the left one peters out and the right crack leans away. At the crux, you have to lean over, slightly off balance, and work your way about three feet horizontally to get to the right crack. That second crack takes you up to about 300 feet above the deck.

As I looked at it that day with Cyndy, it scared me. I just didn't think I could do it. It's not a super hard climb, but as I remembered how much foot smearing on the wall it required, I just wasn't sure I was ready.

It wasn't until the summer of 2011 that I finished that climb again. It was just as fun as I had remembered, but if it tells you anything about the footwork it required, I actually wore the rubber off the front of my prosthetic foot.

It was a poignant moment as I finished. I was powerfully aware of how much time had passed, and how much had happened since 1992. Back then I was just a kid, a young punk with the whole world in front of him. Nineteen years had passed. I'd changed a lot. Immeasurably, in fact, but the rock hadn't changed at all. This time I had the film crew from *The Season* above me recording the whole process, and I felt strong and happy to be back on a climb that meant so much to the younger me.

Moreover, Serenity was the last climb on my original list. I couldn't help being moved as I realized, almost nine years to the day after my accident, I'd reached the goal of doing all the things I had done before, but in a different body.

#7 Yosemite, El Capitan, The Nose—Summer 2011

This particular climb wasn't on the original list, but by all rights it should have been.

At 3,100 vertical feet, The Nose is the longest rock climb in North America, and technically one of the hardest. Because of that, it is the yardstick by which people measure whether someone is truly a "real climber." Do that climb, and you get instant street cred.

The first amputee to climb The Nose in a day.

I'd first climbed on The Nose in 1992, when I was twenty-seven. I did it with a group of three other guys on a route called Triple Direct, which is comprised of The Nose, The Salathe, and the Muir Wall, linking three very famous climbs.

On that first trip, it was a planned five-day climb. Toward the end of the third or fourth day though, a really bad storm came in, and all of us hunkered down on a small ledge to try to wait it out about 600 feet below the rim of El Cap.

Around 11:00 that night, two Spanish climbers came up on us, wearing shorts and t-shirts. They were trying to complete the whole climb in a day, but one would have thought they were really just trying to get themselves killed. They were a train wreck. After more than sixteen hours of climbing, they were hypothermic, tired, and had pretty much nothing in the food and water department.

We told them to stay there with us on the ledge, which was pretty generous considering how small it was and that there were four of us on it already. We also gave them food, water, and extra clothing to try to keep them warm.

What followed was a night that could only be described as horrific. The storm battered at us constantly, making sleep impossible. At one point, one of the Spaniards got so delusional from fatigue and hypothermia that he tried to unhook one of my friends from his tether and push him off. None of us even wanted to try to sleep after that.

As dawn broke, we thought one of the Spaniards had died in the night. A ton of snow had been dumped on the summit and the temperature was around freezing. Try as we might, we couldn't get the guy to wake up.

I don't know what time it was when the helicopter appeared, but the park service, knowing there were climbers on the rock, had gone to check on everyone they could find since the storm was such a freak. As they hovered in front of us, yelling out to ask if we needed help, we made absolutely certain they understood the answer was yes. The search-and-rescue guy nodded and told us to sit tight. An hour later, a team of rescuers dropped down to us from the summit and got us all out of there. By then we'd managed to revive the guy we'd thought was dead, much to our relief, but we soon learned we'd been the lucky ones. The storm that had hit us had come out of nowhere and caught a lot of people unprepared. Two people really had died that night on another part of El Cap.

When I returned to The Nose in 2011, I was with Hans again. The plan was to do it in a day. He already had the speed record for climbing The Nose in a day so I knew I was with the right guy to do it, and not likely to share the fate of the two Spaniards.

It was about 3:00 in the afternoon when I found myself standing once more on that small ledge. It was surreal. The contrast between then and now was almost overpowering. The last time I'd stood there,

I'd been thinking things were about as bad as they could possibly get for me. Now, all these years later, I really knew how much worse things could get. And yet here I was, older, wiser, much more in control and, once again, so incredibly thankful for everything my life had become.

———

There was one climb that was never part of The List.

It couldn't be, because it wasn't like any of the others. It couldn't really be planned, even though I thought about it a lot, because I never knew where, or if, it would happen. The only thing it had in common with the others on The List was that it was more symbolic than anything else, but in its own way, it might have been more important than all the others. And when it finally did happen it was, of all places, in the climbing gym.

I was there by myself, just practicing, when I saw a man being lowered by his son. His back was to me, but as I watched I knew there could be no mistaking who it was coming down the rope. It was Steve Gorham.

That wasn't the first time we'd seen each other since I'd left the hospital, or even since the operation. We'd gotten together with our wives for dinner a couple times, and once in Wyoming he happened to be hiking by while Cyndy and I were out climbing together. We'd all chatted for a bit and then gone our separate ways, but I'll never forget how he choked up a little when he saw that I was climbing again, and climbing well.

That night in the gym the accident was eight years in the past, but as I walked over and shook hands with Steve it was not completely behind us. More talking about it again wasn't going to change anything either, nor was that the place. Instead, we just did what climbers do when they meet up. They invited me to join them.

It was a surreal moment as we headed over to the wall and tied in together for the first time since that nightmare in Estes Park. I climbed first while Steve was on belay, and neither of us had dry eyes as I started up.

I finished the route in a couple minutes, feeling the weirdness of the event the whole way, until I clipped into the anchor and looked down.

Steve's eyes met mine, and there it was. Full circle.

"I've got you," he said. And I knew he did.

I reached the ground, perfectly safe, a few seconds later and we took turns belaying each other for the next couple hours. Neither of us said a word about what was happening, but we both knew it was something powerful and deeply profound.

When the night was over and it was time to part, we talked about getting together again sometime, but as fate would have it both our lives got busy and that night at the gym was the last time we climbed together. Even so, I hope there's no doubt about whether I'd climb with Steve again, inside the gym or out in God's creation. I tell anybody who asks me that question the same thing. Yes, I would.

So is it over? I ask myself that a lot. What happens when you get to the end of a list? Do you make a second? A third? Yes, but for me it was never really about completing a list or checking things off it. It was about challenging myself in a way no one else could. If I ended it with the original list, the fun would end too.

The truth is I need The List. In a weird way, it makes me a better person because it makes me work that much harder at going beyond the "limitations" of my body. It focuses me on something that makes

all the rest of the world melt away. When I'm working on The List I don't hurt as much. I don't think about all the things the accident took from me, or might still take. Instead, I can think about what I've gained from it, and how every inch I climb is a testament to God's amazing power to heal, to love, and to take care of me. When I experience those moments, I appreciate everything more—my wife, my kids, and the gift that we all share in another day of life, all supported by my faith and my knowledge that God has a plan for my life. None of the climbs or any part of my recovery could have come from anywhere else. It's Him I put at the top of The List. After that, it's all joy, and I know I'm going in the right direction.

And so I keep climbing, knowing the top is out there, but never in a hurry to reach it.

At the first All-Disabled Ascent of El Capitan in Yosemite, June 2012.

In Paris, France, to participate in the Paraclimbing World Championships, September 2012. Competing against sixty other climbers, Craig was the only American to advance to the finals, where he won the bronze.

Will, Cyndy, and Mayah on a family climb in El Dorado State Park, 2012.

ABOUT THE AUTHORS

CRAIG DEMARTINO

Since 1994 Craig has journeyed throughout America, Europe, Vietnam, and Israel as the photographer for Group Publishing in Fort Collins, Colorado. Though he continues to shoot pictures for Group Publishing, Craig now also travels throughout the country sharing his story with others, transmitting the powerful message God preserved his life to deliver.

Craig's incredible recovery, documented in the video *After the Fall: A Climber's True Story of Facing Death and Relying on God*, has touched and changed the lives of thousands. National audiences have also been inspired by hearing Craig's dramatic story featured on Discovery Channel's *Vital Scan* series, which won a Gold Telly Award. He has also been featured on CNN and NPR.

In June of last year, he, along with Group Publishing, released Gripping Point, a six-part Bible study based on the topic of pain and how to deal with it in our lives. Craig also tours the country speaking to groups about his accident and the things he has seen God do through the pain he lives with every day, and how to move on after such heavy trauma.

Craig is now climbing again, despite having a leg amputated as a result of the accident. He is the first amputee to ever climb Yosemite's El Capitan and has won five gold medals in climbing competitions at the Extremity Games, with more in his sights.

Craig has also launched After the Fall Ministry, working with other trauma survivors and speaking to groups about his experience of how God used His love to change Craig's heart. He recently released a DVD and ministry guide to complement his speaking and outreach.

BILL ROMANELLI

Bill Romanelli is a professional freelance writer who regularly covers a host of topics from business to the arts, lifestyle, and outdoors. That's in addition to the numerous stories, guest commentaries, and op-ed articles he develops and publishes on behalf of clients in his career as a public relations professional. He has written two other books: *Terminal Velocity* (Christian fiction) and *Life Is Pursuit of the Dream . . .* (teen romance). He was also a contributor to Pastor Ray Johnston's Book, *Help! I'm a Sunday School Teacher!* He and his wife, Janet, live in Northern California, where in addition to writing he works as a public affairs consultant and tries to maintain a healthy balance between work, a passion for all things outdoors, and a hopeless addiction to vanilla chai lattes.